SNAPPED

INSIDE THE MIND OF A COVERT NARCISSIST

SNAPPED

INSIDE THE MIND OF A COVERT NARCISSIST

Esquire Publications
13720 Old Saint Augustine Road #8-322
Jacksonville, FL 32258-7414
www.esquirepublications.com
Tel: 1-800-501-7640

"SNAPPED: Inside the Mind of a Covert Narcissist"

Edited By: Georgia Editing Service, LLC

Typeset and Cover Design By: Designs Unparallel, LLC
www.designsunparallel.com

Library of Congress Control Number: 2025934908
ISBN: 979-8-9900739-5-1

Introduction

As a Counselor and survivor, it is essential to explain narcissism, as understanding this personality disorder is vital for healing and preventing further harm. Narcissistic behavior can often be subtle and manipulative, leaving survivors feeling confused, self-blaming, or trapped in unhealthy cycles. By educating everyone about the traits of narcissism – such as lack of empathy, manipulation, and a need for control – I aim to empower others and survivors to recognize these behaviors in their own experiences and relationships.

This knowledge is crucial for establishing healthy boundaries, rebuilding self-esteem, and fostering emotional resilience. For survivors, gaining insight into narcissism helps shift the focus from self-blame to accountability for the narcissist's actions, clarifying why certain patterns occurred. As a result, survivors are better equipped to make informed decisions, protect their mental and emotional well-being, and heal from the psychological damage caused by narcissistic abuse.

In the pages that follow, I studied the intricate landscape of covert narcissism, a psychological phenomenon that captivates and challenges our understanding of human behavior. This exploration is not just an academic pursuit, but a journey sparked by my personal experiences, particularly with the complex realm of marriage.

This book seeks to unravel layers, offering insights into the facets of covert narcissistic traits, the impact on individuals and relationships, and the profound influence that covert narcissism can wield in both personal and societal contexts.

As I navigate this exploration, I invite you to reflect on your encounters with covert narcissism, whether in personal relationships or the broader spheres of life. I aim to foster a deeper comprehension of this complex aspect of human psychology by understanding the nuances of covert narcissistic behaviors.

Prepare to embark on an exhilarating expedition that combines personal anecdotes, psychological analysis, and a quest for greater awareness. This book endeavors not only to unravel the intricacies of covert narcissism but also to spark conversations that can lead to personal growth, empathy, and a more profound understanding of the human psyche.

You can know someone your whole life, yet they can still be strangers...

Elva Chase, BCCC

Before I dive into my story, I want to be fully transparent with you. This book is based on my husband of seven and a half years, Earl—who is also one of my older first cousins, five years my senior. Our mothers are half-sisters (same mother, different fathers). Earl and I grew up together, but we lived separate lives as time passed. We married, had children, and moved to different states. We hadn't seen each other since 1996. All I remembered of Earl was that he was sweet, funny, kind, respectful, and protective. He was always someone I admired and looked up to. Never in a million years did I think Earl would ever do me *"like that,"* let alone my children, because we were family. However, what you're about to read is something I never saw coming.

In 2017, while strolling through social media, a random profile popped up. You know how that goes—profiles you don't have to be friends with. The photo caught my eye: it was Earl, and the caption said, "We don't get to pick our parents, but I'm glad you're my dad. Happy Birthday." I realized it was his daughter's account. Curious, I zoomed in on the picture to confirm it was him, and as I scrolled through more of her posts, I saw pictures of his brother and his dad. I decided to reach out, introducing myself as his cousin and explaining how we were related. I asked about Earl's whereabouts, and she told me he was in prison in South Carolina. She even gave me his address.

From that moment on, Earl and I began writing letters, reconnecting about our lives, families, and fond childhood memories. It didn't take long for us to transition from letters to phone calls, where I'd set up my phone so Earl could call me directly. We spoke every day—sometimes multiple times a day—sharing stories about our divorces and our kids, and eventually, Earl opened up about why he was incarcerated. He explained that he had brutally beaten his wife after discovering that she was running, as well as participating in a brothel at the gas station/truck stop where she worked. He had suspected something was off because of the extra money she was bringing home and the rumors swirling around. Although I understood that what Earl did was wrong and domestic violence is never acceptable, I couldn't reconcile it with the sweet, protective cousin I remembered. I had experienced abuse myself in a past marriage, so it wasn't lost on me how serious this was, but still, in my mind, Earl was family, and I struggled to align this version of him with the one I had known.

Our daily calls continued, and eventually, I began making weekend trips to visit Earl in prison. Our conversations were mostly about family—reminiscing about old times and remembering funny stories about our parents, grandparents, and siblings. Over time, however, our relationship deepened, and we became more than just family reconnecting.

When I made my kids aware of how close Earl and I had become, Prince and Mona were immediately supportive, but Alexis was more cautious. She wasn't sure about our bond and decided to do some biblical research to ensure everything lined up. She was skeptical until she found a few facts in the Bible about close relatives marrying, which helped her understand our situation.

For instance:
* **Elizabeth and Zechariah**, the parents of John the Baptist, are described in the Gospel of Luke as relatives of Mary, the mother of Jesus. The word "suggenēs" is used, which generally means "kinswoman" or "relative," often interpreted as cousins.
* **Mary and Joseph:** Although the Bible doesn't explicitly state that Mary, the mother of Jesus, and Joseph were cousins, some traditions and interpretations suggest they may have been closely related by kinship. However, this connection is less clear from the biblical text itself.

* **Isaac and Rebekah** were first cousins once removed. Rebekah was the daughter of Bethuel, who was the cousin of Isaac's father, Abraham.

*__Jacob, later named Israel, married both Leah and Rachel__, who were sisters and cousins. They were daughters of Laban, who was Jacob's uncle.

* **Amram and Jochebed**, the parents of Moses, were also closely related, possibly cousins, though this is inferred from Jewish tradition rather than explicitly stated in the Bible.

Though the Bible doesn't specifically endorse marriages between cousins, there are examples of closely related individuals marrying, especially in the Old Testament.

Marriages That God Prohibits

Forbidden Marriages	Passage
Between mother and son. (Note that sexual relations between father and daughter are prohibited by Leviticus 18:6 and 21:2-3)	Leviticus 18:7-8
With stepchildren.	Leviticus 18:17
With an aunt.	Leviticus 18:12-14
With sister or half-sister.	Leviticus 18:9; Deuteronomy 27:22
With half-sister and stepsisters.	Leviticus 18:11
With daughter-in-law.	Leviticus 18:15
With your sister-in-law.	Leviticus 18:16
With your granddaughter.	Leviticus 18:10
With your step-granddaughter.	Leviticus 18:17

This list includes those found in Leviticus 20:11-21;
Deuteronomy 22:30; Deuteronomy 27:20-23; and 1 Corinthians
5:1.

Although people may judge our union as "wrong" or "not
of Christ," I respect their views. I'm not trying to justify
anything but rather share my story.

The purpose of this book is to shed light on narcissism
and the different forms it takes, including where it comes from.
It's not just about Earl and me. Narcissism happens in all kinds
of relationships—marriages, co-workers, friends, and even
among siblings and parents.

WHAT IS A COVERT NARCISSIST & HOW TO IDENTIFY ONE?

A covert narcissist is someone who craves admiration and a sense of importance while lacking empathy for others. Unlike overt narcissists, who openly display their traits, covert narcissists conceal their behaviors, making them more difficult to identify. Despite their reserved or modest outward demeanor, their underlying motivations align with typical narcissistic traits, such as self-importance, fantasies of fame or glory, a desire for admiration, exploitation of others, and a disregard for others' feelings.

Recognizing a covert narcissist involves observing both the overt and subtler behaviors associated with narcissistic personality disorder (NPD). While a clinical diagnosis requires meeting specific criteria, everyday interactions can reveal common signs like a lack of empathy, manipulation, and exploitation. Understanding these traits empowers individuals to navigate potentially unhealthy relationships more effectively, as covert narcissism can be just as harmful as its more obvious counterparts.

Causes of Covert Narcissism

The exact causes of covert narcissism are not entirely understood, but several factors likely contribute. Experts suggest that narcissistic personality disorder is linked to factors including:

- Genetics
- Childhood abuse and trauma
- Upbringing and relationships with caregivers
- Personality and temperament

One study found that people with narcissistic personality disorder are more likely to have grown up with parents who were highly focused on status and achievements.

Because they were often made to feel superior to other children, the belief that they are special and more valuable than others may persist into adulthood.

SYMPTOMS
of Narcissistic Personality Disorder

Considers themself intelligent, confident, and self-assured

Believes they are unique and special

Is unable to empathize

Has a grandiose sense of self

Always thinks they're right

Manipulates, blames, and gaslights

Has an excessive need for praise and admiration

Displays a sense of entitlement

Uses criticism and bullying to achieve their goals

What Triggers a Covert Narcissist?

It is not clear, however, why narcissistic behavior is sometimes displayed in covert rather than overt ways. Some situations that might trigger a covert narcissist include:

- *Being ignored*
- *Feeling disrespected*
- *Threats to their ego*
- *Feelings of shame*
- *Being around high-status people*
- *Feeling less attractive or less educated than others*
- *Having less of something than others*
- *Not getting the attention they think they deserve*
- *Jealousy*
- *Lack of control*

(*Lately, Earl's moods had become unpredictable, shifting from hot to warm to ice-cold in an instant. It felt like anything could set him off, and walking on eggshells had become a way of life. Our home was no longer a refuge—it was tense, divided, and suffocating. Mona and Prince were visibly unhappy, retreating to their rooms for most of the day if they weren't at work.*

Family dinners became a thing of the past—instead of sitting together, they would grab their plates and eat in isolation. I only heard them laugh when they were alone together, away from Earl's presence. When I tried to talk to them to see what was wrong, they would shake their heads, offering nothing but silence. But I knew better. I know my children, and I refused to accept their silence as truth. When I pressed them again, they finally admitted what I already feared—they weren't happy. Earl was always yelling at them, blaming them, or finding something to be angry about.

I wanted to believe there was some misunderstanding, but there wasn't. I saw it. I felt it. I knew exactly what they were going through because I was experiencing it, too. I tried to mediate, defend, and restore peace. I even suggested family counseling, but it only led to more conflict. Whenever we tried to hold a family meeting, Earl would storm off in a rage, unwilling to listen.

Something had to change.

So, I did the only thing I knew to do—I prayed. I decided to FAST, writing down every intention on my list, including one that weighed the heaviest on my heart: "Peace in our home." The very next morning, Earl woke up in a bad mood. And that was the day everything unraveled.)

The September 1, 2023, memory remains etched in my mind, a day we will never forget. It's the day when my twins saved my life from their stepfather and barely escaped with their own. Even now, I find myself replaying the events of that day in my mind repeatedly, unable to fully digest all that has transpired.

MAKING FALSE ACCUSATIONS/BLAME

When a narcissist feels like they are losing control or like they are in the mood to stir up drama and create chaos, they might exaggerate conflicts, fabricate situations, or make false accusations. They want to provoke guilt, confusion, and emotional distress in you. If you deny, defend, or justify yourself, you will give them exactly what they want: A reaction.

As I awoke to the eerie sound of Earl whispering to himself, his words low and fragmented as if engaged in a secret conversation, an unsettling tension hung heavy in the air that morning, gripping me with an unshakable sense of dread. I could already sense Earl's negative energy. It wasn't even 8 AM yet, so I couldn't fathom why he was in a sour mood. Following my usual routine, I attempted to diffuse conflict by kissing him on the forehead, offering a cheerful good morning, and beginning my morning prayer. Normally, he would join me in prayer, kneeling beside me, but lately, he'd merely kneeled on his side of the bed, hands unfurled, appearing impatient. It seemed as if he didn't even participate in the prayers. He remained motionless, looking around until I finished, then retreated to bed in silence, covers pulled up, staring blankly ahead. His demeanor, cold and distant, ignored my greetings and affectionate gestures. His behavior signaled yet another challenging encounter. It was too early for such tension.

The previous evening, everything seemed fine. We enjoyed a great movie, snuggled in bed, indulged in snacks, shared laughter, and engaged in a pleasant discussion afterward. We cuddled and conversed until we drifted off to sleep. Yet, with him, it always felt like any moment of happiness was fleeting.

(*Not all our times together were bad. We experienced awesome, fun times. After Earl's release, finding employment was challenging due to his felonies and parole status, so I welcomed him into my publishing company I have nurtured for 14 years and counting, giving him an opportunity to rebuild and move forward. He was my Director of Sales, for which he was compensated bi-weekly. His responsibilities included reaching out to local bookstores across diverse locations to organize book signings and secure shelf space for our authors.*

Some of these book signing events required us to travel out of state, flying to attend and support our authors. It was my duty as the Publisher. Earl received permission from his parole officer for each trip and was granted a travel permit every time. We even went so far as to get family passports, as he only had a few years left on parole, and we were planning family trips abroad.

I also extended him a position with our then-employment staffing agency. Alexis and I partnered for over 10 years, a venture that was deeply affected by the economic downturn brought on by COVID-19. As many of our clients' businesses closed, we ultimately made the difficult decision to dissolve the company in 2022. Within the agency, Earl worked as a Talent Acquisition Manager, again, with a bi-weekly salary, responsible for conducting initial phone interviews with potential candidates. The process was structured—Alexis handled all our Human Resource activities, Mona and Prince were the Talent Acquisition Specialists who sourced qualified applicants and forwarded their resumes to Earl, who would then screen them, evaluate their credentials, interview performance, and determine whether they were fit for a second-round interview with me. I was the Recruiter and would then conduct the final interview before presenting them to our clients for hire.

Beyond business, Earl was also involved in my nonprofit organization, which I have led for 15 years and counting. Together, we traveled to different cities, responding to requests from families and communities needing clothing, furniture, and groceries. While my organization is primarily a domestic violence agency, I also operate a mobile food pantry and caring closet of apparel and furniture, where the public can submit online applications through the website to request assistance.

Earl was involved in many aspects of my life and businesses, and at one point, we even purchased a home together, with Mona as our Realtor. We often shared meaningful moments as a family, like holding Bible studies *weekly, gathering in a circle, and holding hands of taking turns praying every morning and night.*

Earl and Prince sometimes had heart-to-heart conversations and would spend time shopping at the mall. We all cherished family movie and game nights, sharing laughs over card and board games and enjoying family manicures and pedicures together.

Our outings were truly unforgettable, from traveling with Alexis to professional football games, ziplining, golfing, fishing, horseback riding, and weekend trips to different states for special events. Even simple tasks like going to the supermarket became a group affair, with Mona often walking arm-in-arm with Earl while Prince strolled alongside him on the other side. Prince would mimic Earl's gestures, like opening doors for us, and after grocery runs, he'd eagerly help Earl carry and put away the groceries. When we weren't shopping or at the movies, Earl, Mona, and Prince would jog together, or we would play basketball in teams.

We were introduced by Prince, who was active in modeling activewear apparel and T-shirt brands for clothing companies on Instagram and became ambassador models as well. Prince also explored content creation on YouTube and often featured Earl in his skits. Prince was also an actor working on his second movie in which the director gave Earl a small role. We even renewed our then-5th-year wedding anniversary with a ceremony in our pool home. Our plan was to renew our vows every year instead of every five or 10 years.

Memories like these made how it all ended even more heartbreaking. The twins truly believed they had a 'real dad' they could look up to, and I thought I'd finally found my 'happily ever after.' Earl was home to me. Emotionally, he gave me some of that "up home" type feeling that I missed from being around my family members, and that made me trust him, and I felt safe with him. A familiar soul. In my mind, because of who we were, I thought I never had to worry about being cheated on or physically abused like in my first marriage. But that's how narcissists operate—they wear a mask until it eventually falls off.)

Earl seemed to stir up drama over trivial matters, and I wanted no part of it. Choosing to start my day, I showered and grabbed my laptop to check my emails.

While I typically worked from the comfort of my bed, I preferred to avoid his company since he had the day off from his finally new job. His days off often brought tension. Without something to occupy him, arguments were inevitable. He always seemed to find something to accuse the twins of, and I wasn't in the mood to hear it again. Before I could even leave the bathroom, he barged in, accusingly stating,

"Yesterday, I noticed all the white socks I bought were missing from my drawer. But when I went into Mona's room to drop off some clean laundry, I saw a few pairs of them on her dresser." Mona, my then 19-year-old daughter, was the twin sister to my son, Prince.

"Why would she steal my socks when I always buy her several pair?" he demanded.

"I don't think she stole anything; if she wants something, she always asks, and you know that," I replied.

Moreover, I admitted fault, acknowledging that I also placed laundry in Mona's room, confusing whose socks were whose. Still, Earl remained adamant, claiming Mona deliberately took his socks to spite him despite having no evidence. I urged him to stop accusing her without proof, but he stormed into her room, flicking on her bright overhead light and waking her with his accusations. Mona denied taking the socks, but Earl persisted, leaving in anger.

Returning to our room, Earl's fury turned towards me, insisting Mona manipulated me, that she was trying to control me, and that she was lying. He remained fixated on the socks, yelling while clenching his shaking fists, veins popping out of his head, "My SOOOCCKKKSSSS!!!" even after I explained my mistake. This incident left him seething, and Mona, likely hearing his tirade, gathered all the socks he'd ever bought her and bagged them up for donation.

Earl then shifted the blame to Prince,

"Oh yeah, you need to talk to your son about locking the door when he leaves for work." Prince worked the wee hours of the morning at the airport from 4 AM to 12 PM. We had a ring doorbell, and the app was on our cell phones.

"You know I'm watching him on the camera to ensure he locks the door. I had to go downstairs a few times, and the door was wide open." Earl exaggeratedly stated. "He probably left it open when he was falling asleep standing at the door," he said while laughing at the fact that Prince was falling asleep.

"If you saw him falling asleep, why didn't you tell me? That's dangerous; he could fall asleep at the wheel on his way to work!" I exclaimed.

"It's not my responsibility; he thinks he's grown; he'll be all right." He spoke.

"We live in a gated community; you can't get in without codes," I said.

"So, what you tryna say?" he said angrily while raising his voice.

"Why don't you tell him?" I suggested.

"If I tell him, it's going to be a problem!" he exclaimed.

"Why does it have to be a problem just to tell him to make sure he locks the door when he leaves?" I asked.

"You heard what I said, make sure you tell him!" he demanded.

I texted Prince, asking him to lock the door when he left for work. He texted back, letting me know that he always locks the door. I checked the ring camera unbeknownst to Earl and saw Prince closing and using his key to lock the door. I even ran the camera back to past days and weeks, and Prince was right…he ALWAYS locked the door. I could hear the click of the lock on the camera. I didn't want Prince to know where that suggestion came from, so I apologized, thanked him for "always" locking the door and told him I would buy him some energy drinks to assist with the tiredness.

Earl continued his tirade, blaming my children, referring to them as "your f***ing kids!!!" and suggesting they go live with their absent father despite knowing the complexities of their relationship. His unfounded accusations and volatile behavior escalated, all before 9 AM.

HIGHLY SENSITIVE TO CRITICISM

Those with narcissism are usually insecure and have easily damaged self-esteem. Thus, when someone criticizes the covert narcissist, they may make dismissive, sarcastic, and defensive comments to deflect the criticism.

Earl and I used to have regular date nights with Mona, selecting a fancy restaurant. This became a bi-monthly tradition for us, starting off sweetly as we dressed up and posed for pictures taken by Prince before our family evening prayer and departure. We never stayed out too late, often returning home well before midnight. We limited our alcohol intake to one glass of wine each, with me typically being the designated driver.

However, I noticed a change during these outings. Earl started adding two glasses of wine with a shot of liquor, and as the night progressed, his behavior became more erratic. He would repeatedly boast about his appearance and then transition into senseless questioning and baseless accusations about my past high school guy friendships, insinuating that I "slept" with them. Despite my honest responses, he persisted, refusing to believe me and causing unnecessary arguments.

On one particularly controversial night, fueled by alcohol, our arguing became loud and heated. Despite my reservations, Earl had convinced me to keep alcohol in the house, promising to limit his intake to one glass per night with dinner. However, that evening escalated, with us consuming far more than intended. Earl began berating two of my then-estranged daughters, accusing them of being evil, just wanting to use me, and not loving or caring about me or their siblings, which led to a shouting match. When Mona intervened, expressing her discomfort with Earl's behavior, stating that he was "unpredictable" when he drank, he lashed out at her, accusing her of disrespect and suggesting she didn't care about me either.

Attempting to defuse Earl's escalating tension and disliking hurtful comments about my daughters, I intervened and urged him and Mona to stop. However, Mona continued to yell back at Earl, disregarding my pleas for peace. Desperate to quiet her down, I ended up in a pulling/pushing altercation with

Mona, a moment I deeply regretted. It was particularly distressing as Mona, who has never disrespected me, was involved. Eventually, Prince stepped in, pulling me away from Mona, while Earl remained passive, silently observing before walking away.

With Earl gone, the three of us were left in tears. We reconciled and spent hours sitting together, crying, and holding each other. I apologized profusely for my actions, feeling like a failure as a mother. Later, as I lay in bed, Earl played pool in the garage, but I chose to remain in bed, ignoring him. Eventually, he joined me, but we lay there in silence, our backs turned to each other.

Mona sent me a heartfelt text during the night expressing her hurt over the events and the altercation. I apologized sincerely, feeling immense guilt. She came into the room, and we spent the night holding each other, both in tears.

As morning approached, Earl questioned Mona's presence in our room, but I firmly asserted her right to talk about her feelings. Despite Earl's dismissive attitude, Mona and I supported each other. Eventually, Mona returned to her bed, and we attempted to move forward from the tumultuous night.

Later that morning, Earl approached my side of the bed, informing me he had something to confess.

"Go ahead," I responded, though I couldn't bring myself to look at him.

"Last night, I slashed Mona's tires...all four. I was angry because I felt she disrespected me by calling me unpredictable when I drink, so I felt she didn't deserve to drive." He admitted. I was speechless, my mind racing about immediately rectifying this situation. Mona didn't even know yet. How would she react? What could I do? I was utterly flabbergasted. I looked at Earl, unable to find the words. Running the security footage on my cell phone, I watched in utter disbelief as Earl punctured each tire with a kitchen knife.

"Have you told her?" I asked.

"No, but I told Prince," He replied.

"And what did he say?" I inquired.

"Prince said, 'Whoa!'" Earl recounted how he had confessed to Prince when apologizing for the previous night's events.

"You need to speak to Mona immediately; she has work tomorrow morning," I instructed Earl. He called for Mona to join us in our bedroom, apologizing for the previous night's altercation and revealing what he had done to her car. Mona sat silently, her eyes fixed on the floor, clearly zoned off.

This was a devastating revelation, and I felt like an absolute failure. This car, a convertible little beetle, was Mona's pride and joy, purchased entirely with her saved hard-earned money from her job at the carwash where she and Prince worked at the time. Despite Earl's apology, he immediately followed up with, "I didn't appreciate you calling me unpredictable," as if to justify his actions. I shared Mona's skeptical look as I interrupted our stare-down to turn to her, instructing her to get dressed because we were heading to Walmart to replace all four tires. We swiftly took care of this, which lifted her spirits, and we ended the day with Mona's favorite activity: a trip to the ice cream shop. Mona forgave Earl and maintained a polite demeanor, but little did he know that their emotional rift had already begun.

ENVY

People with covert narcissism often feel envy of others who have things that they think they are entitled to themselves. They may not outwardly express their envy but may show bitterness or resentment towards others. Similarly, they believe that other people envy them because of the belief that they are special.

Earl and I strolled through downtown on one of our evenings out, enjoying the cityscape. At his insistence, we paused at a quaint café for a light meal, accompanied by what was meant to be a single glass of wine. However, Earl deviated from the plan, opting for three glasses of Merlot and a tall beer. Moderation was no longer his strong suit. When I cautioned him against overindulging, his (*"I'm good"*) response always rang hollow, signaling his disregard for caution. As the hour grew late, I called Prince to pick us up. Twenty minutes passed, and we heard a loud crash—it was Prince. Another car had cut in front of him, resulting in a collision. Fortunately, no one was injured, including Mona and older sibling, Alexis, who was also in the car.

With Prince's car deemed totaled, we all had to Uber home. The next day, I filed a claim with our insurance company, who generously compensated Prince for his loss. I suggested he invest in a BMW because I wanted him to have something nice. At the dealership, we found a suitable BMW. Earl frequently requested the car keys, often making snide remarks regarding Prince's possession of a BMW with a mix of resentment and feigned admiration. Aside from his outburst of *"I can't believe this little n**ga got a BMW!!!"* I could sense the underlying irritation in his tone, particularly when he repeated his ignorant statement multiple times. It became apparent that Earl's words lacked sincerity and were driven more by obligation than genuine sentiment.

One evening, Earl indulged in drinks at home, but his lack of moderation always led to intoxication and subsequent arguments. Despite his apologies the next day, promising not to drink again, even removing alcohol from our home, he would inevitably return to it after about a month. Following his drinking episodes, Earl would often feel compelled to drive. Taking the car keys, he would head out, leaving me worried and frantically calling him to come home. Despite my pleas and warnings about the dangers of drinking and driving, he wouldn't heed my advice.

Late into the wee hours of the night, I spent hours calling and begging him to return, especially before the twins woke up to volunteer at a downtown marathon. I dreaded facing them if they asked about Earl's absence. Mona and Prince entered my bedroom as morning approached to inform me, they were heading to the marathon. Prince inquired about Earl's whereabouts,

"Where's Pops?" asked Prince. I could only reply with embarrassment,

"I don't know, Son."

I explained how every time I called him, he sounded intoxicated or abruptly hung up. Despite their reassurances that 'Pops' would return soon; I couldn't shake off the worry weighing heavily on my mind.

After several hours, the twins contacted me to let me know they were on their way home. I asked them to drive around and check if they could spot Earl driving our truck, as the GPS tracker we were all using showed he was downtown. They agreed and promised to call if they spotted him. Barely 20 minutes had passed before they called back. Mona reported,

"We pulled up beside Pop at a light, and I got out and knocked on his window. He seemed surprised, then angry. There was some dirty-looking guy in the car with him. I told him you wanted him to come home."

Unfortunately, their encounter seemed to have little impact on Earl, who arrived home after the twins. It was well past 9 AM when he finally returned, apologizing, and claiming he had been driving around town to sober up. When questioned about the stranger in the car, he explained that he had given him a ride, bought him beer and cigarettes, and dropped him off at his girlfriend's place.

I was filled with disgust and anger. Picking up strangers posed a severe risk; he put his life in danger, and not to mention our personal information was accessible in the glove compartment. I expressed my frustration and concern over the recklessness of his actions. Earl's apologies rang hollow, as they often did, given his pattern of repeating the same behavior despite his remorse.

Not long after the previous incident, Earl had another drunken episode, which went too far this time. He entered Prince's bedroom and took his car keys without asking. As he stumbled into our bedroom, Prince followed closely behind, learning of Earl's actions. Prince asked Earl if he had seen his keys, and Earl lied, denying any knowledge of them. When Prince asked me for confirmation, I honestly replied that I hadn't seen them either, as I had no idea what Earl had done. Frustrated, Prince returned to his room and shut the door. Shortly after, Earl left the house, and within less than fifteen minutes, I received a distressing phone call. It was Earl informing me that he was with the police because he had crashed Prince's car into a pole, totaling it.

According to the officer, Earl claimed that he and I had been arguing, and in his upset state, he lost control of the car. Remarkably, no arrest was made due to the officer's understanding of the situation and Earl's intoxicated state. I woke Mona and Prince and went to the accident scene, witnessing Prince's devastation firsthand. The officer showed us grace and understanding of the circumstances, but Earl seemed oblivious to the magnitude of his actions.

The drive home was somber, with Mona, Prince, and me left speechless. Earl complained of pain in his knee and elbow, lamenting how he could have lost his life. We remained silent, feeling fed up with his repeated apologies for his drunken behavior and the chaos he caused.

Upon arriving home, Mona and Prince quietly retreated to their rooms and closed their doors. Filled with lingering questions about the accident, I confronted Earl, asking him why he had taken Prince's car, why he had chosen to drink and drive, and why he hadn't even apologized to Prince. I didn't hold back, expressing my concerns about his behavior towards Prince, particularly his jealous remarks. Earl laughed at my concerns, dismissing my suggestions of jealousy as absurd and insisting that he loved Prince as his son.

The following morning, Earl entered the kitchen, his eyes filled with tears as he struggled to apologize, but his remorse was directed solely towards me. I insisted he needed to apologize to Prince, but I knew his repeated apologies had lost their sincerity to the children, as well as myself. Prince began avoiding Earl, choosing to eat his meals in his room or with Mona, who remained cordial but reserved. Understanding their discomfort, I would check in on them, offering a smile, hug, and kiss whenever possible.

Dealing with the aftermath of the accident, I had to navigate through insurance matters, which resulted in a $200 increase in our policy, raising our monthly expenses to over $700. However, the insurance covered the damage entirely, again generously compensating Prince for the loss. Prince decided to purchase a Jeep and kept his car keys hidden in a stuffed bear with a secret compartment, with Mona holding onto the spare key.

To address his drinking problem, Earl decided to attend AA meetings, and I accompanied him for support. While Mona remained hopeful, Prince remained skeptical. Earl's brief commitment to AA crumbled within a month, his return to old habits casting a dark shadow that hinted at something far more sinister lurking beneath the surface.

GASLIGHTING

Gaslighting is a form of psychological abuse or manipulation in which the abuser attempts to sow self-doubt and confusion in the victim's mind.

Below are some examples of gaslighting tactics. Many of these tactics may not be isolated; some may be used in one instance or conversation. The more they are used on someone, the more likely they are to question their reality.

Rewriting History

One gaslighting method people may use is to retell stories that work in their favor.

They could change the story to make the victim look like they are the abusive one. For instance, if a gaslighting partner has been yelling at their spouse all evening to the point where the spouse yells back, the gaslighter may rewrite the story by saying, 'You were yelling at me for no reason.'

The victim may begin to doubt their memories of what happened, the confusion or second-guessing being the exact intent of the gaslighter.

Minimizing

This can involve someone belittling or trivializing the victim's feelings. They may often say, 'You are overreacting' or 'You are too sensitive.'

If they say something hurtful, they may also say, 'I was only joking,' to reinforce that the other person is overreacting. Victims may question whether their concerns and feelings are real or may feel silly for overreacting.

If the victim is dealing with someone who does not acknowledge their thoughts, feelings, or beliefs, they may never feel validated or understood, which can be challenging to cope with.

Denial

A gaslighter may pretend to forget events or how they happened, such as saying, 'That never happened.' They may also accuse the victim of making things up so that the victim appears to be lying.

Even when the victim provides proof of the lies, the gaslighter will not back down and may be very convincing when denying it, even if the victim knows they are lying. This can leave the victim feeling confused, unseen, unheard, and second-guessing themselves.

There are many tactics that gaslighters can use to manipulate their victims into questioning their perceptions of reality, their thoughts, and their feelings.

I reached a breaking point where I felt compelled to limit my outings with Earl because of his inability to keep his focus on us. It didn't matter where we went—whether it was the grocery store, clothing store, gas station, or restaurant—his eyes would wander towards other women. Sometimes, he would even blatantly turn his head to make eye contact with them. When I confronted him about his disrespectful behavior and how it hurt me, his responses were dismissive and defensive. He would claim that he wasn't actively looking at anyone, accuse me of trying to control him, or even gaslight me by denying events that to him had never transpired.

These arguments became a near-daily occurrence, with Earl always finding ways to deflect or deny my concerns. He even went as far as to deny the evidence captured on our Ring Doorbell video, where he was seen turning to look at the FedEx delivery person as she walked away. His response was to invalidate the video and question my sanity for keeping it. This constant cycle of denial and deflection only added to the strain on our marriage.

We found ourselves behind a young couple as we left the grocery store. The man was pushing the cart, and his woman walked beside him. Suddenly, another woman, dressed provocatively, passed them, drawing attention with her revealing attire and somewhat exposed body parts. Despite this, the man remained focused on his conversation with his partner. Earl remarked,

"Wow, he didn't even look; he must really love her." I couldn't help but question him,

"What do you mean by that, considering you always look?" He quickly backtracked, saying,

"Oh, no, I didn't mean anything by it." When I asked if that meant he didn't love me, he dismissed it with a sigh,

"Come on, what kind of question is that? You already know, so don't start." He then brought up a nonexistent incident of me gawking at other men, a claim I refuted as I've always respected myself as a married woman and mother. Despite my concerns, Earl often tried to deflect or deny his behavior, leaving me unheard and disrespected.

He constantly gaslighted me, making me doubt my perceptions by denying his actions. Sometimes, I questioned whether I was overreacting, which frustrated me. His constant lying and denial wore me down, and I resented how he made me doubt my worth. He began mocking me, making inappropriate comments about my appearance whenever I entered the room. Though I tried to laugh it off along with his laugh because he thought he was funny, his words cut deep, leaving me insecure and self-conscious. His incessant gawking of other women during outings further shattered my self-esteem. It didn't end there; he would often need my help to remove viruses from his devices, resulting from the porn he watched. Despite his apologies and assurances that he wasn't watching it in the way that I believed, I was disgusted and emotionally and mentally exhausted. I felt like I was losing myself, trapped in a cycle of brokenness and despair.

I presented him with the evidence, but he dismissed it, saying, "You didn't see what you think you saw. I wasn't looking at her like that."

PLAYING THE VICTIM

Inducing guilt and playing the victim is a common strategy used by narcissists. A narcissist will exaggerate or fabricate situations to manipulate emotions, gain sympathy, and deflect responsibility for their actions.

Narcissists are skilled at painting a convincing picture of their suffering and luring you into their web of conflict and drama. They might tell you how difficult their life is or how everyone is against them. They might claim that others have mistreated them or that they are constantly misunderstood or unappreciated.

They make others feel responsible for their negative emotions or situations, emphasizing their empathy and desire to help or fix things. They may twist facts, distort reality, or engage in gaslighting to manipulate others into feeling at fault.

Narcissists believe that nobody should be content without them, so they try to drag you down with them.

How to Respond

Narcissists often attract people with high levels of empathy. They rely on your good nature and compassion and know you will find it challenging to resist helping them when needed.

Narcissists are skilled manipulators, making you feel like you owe them in some way or that it would be unkind to ignore them or say no.

But you must remind yourself that their victim-playing and guilt-tripping are only attempts to manipulate and control you emotionally. They are using your vulnerabilities for their gain.

You may believe that you are the only person who can help them. Remember that you are not responsible for the narcissist's emotions or actions.

And know that if they cannot get a response out of you, they will contact someone else. They probably have multiple sources of narcissistic supply.

Responding to a narcissist's victim-playing and guilt-tripping can be challenging, as they may resist or escalate their manipulative tactics. Prioritize your well-being, trust your instincts, and seek professional help. Do not engage with them. Establish clear boundaries and communicate them assertively. Be prepared for resistance or attempts to push those boundaries but remain firm in upholding them.

We all agreed that seeking counseling could help improve our family dynamics. After researching online, I found a counselor, Ms. Sophia, who specializes in adult teens and family therapy. I promptly booked an appointment for the earliest available slot.

On the day of our appointment, I encouraged Mona and Prince to express their feelings openly without holding back. As we sat in the lobby, Ms. Sophia emerged and led us down a long hallway to her office at the end. Mona and Prince sat together on a small sofa while Earl and I settled on the couch.

During introductions, Ms. Sophia inquired about the reason for our visit. I began explaining our desire to enhance communication within the family. However, Earl quickly interjected and dominated the conversation, speaking for most of the allotted hour. I grew increasingly frustrated as he monopolized the discussion, airing grievances about the twins' supposed lack of respect and accusing Mona of speaking for her and Prince. He brought up past incidents, such as the sock incident with Mona and the door-locking issue with Prince, and criticized the twins for not being active enough in caring for our dog. Earl even suggested that they were the main instigators of our arguments and hinted that they should consider moving out.

His one-sided narrative left me feeling unheard and marginalized in the session. It was evident that Earl's perspective overshadowed the opportunity for balanced dialogue and resolution.

Mona and Prince remained silent for the most part, only speaking up when prompted by Ms. Sophia. They shared their reluctance to communicate with Earl, citing his tendency to yell instead of engaging in constructive dialogue. They expressed their dislike for him and recounted the incidents involving their cars, the failed attempt to keep up with AA meetings, and the constant letdown of not keeping his promises of doing better, which strained their relationship with him. Ms. Sophia emphasized to Earl the importance of giving them time to heal from these experiences and how his yelling only pushed them further away. Despite his pretense of understanding, Earl's concern seemed superficial and short-lived.

As tears welled in my eyes, Earl exaggeratedly leaped to fetch a tissue and forced held my hand as if to show support. Failing to see through his fake, sincere gesture, Ms. Sophia explained that I was caught in the middle of the situation, with Earl supposedly trying to protect me. However, it was clear that Earl's actions were more about manipulation than genuine care.

Ms. Sophia suggested that we attend future sessions separately. She proposed seeing Mona and Prince together while Earl and I would undergo marriage counseling. Earl deflected blame over several sessions and presented himself as a victim. I clarified that while Mona and Prince initially wanted him to adopt them and change their last name to his, however, Earl's behavior, particularly his drinking and the incidents with their cars, had caused them to reassess their perception of him as a father figure.

Earl remained silent initially, and Ms. Sophia refrained from entertaining his complaints. However, Earl persisted with his grievances and falsehoods. He attributed everything to Mona and Prince, even going as far as accusing them of hiding his asthma inhaler. Despite my observation of Earl pushing the inhaler aside as if it was hidden underneath linen and later 'miraculously' finding it himself, he blamed the twins, feigning confusion and indignation.

As he continued to spin his narrative to Ms. Sophia, he portrayed himself as a victim in his own home, claiming that he felt marginalized by the twins and me. Finally, I interjected and steered the conversation toward the dog issue. I recounted how Prince had attempted to accommodate Earl's concerns by moving the dog's kennel into his room to prevent her whining from disturbing Earl's sleep. However, Earl had insisted on moving the kennel back into our room, disregarding Prince's effort to resolve the issue amicably. It seemed to me that Earl was intent on perpetuating conflict even when there were attempts to resolve it.

Ms. Sophia directed her question to Earl, inquiring why he had Prince reverse the arrangement with the dog's kennel. Earl's response was a concoction of falsehoods, claiming he didn't want Prince burdened with the responsibility due to his early work schedule *(totally ignoring the gripe Earl previously relayed of having a problem with the twins lacking responsibility for the dog)*. Despite the blatant dishonesty, Ms. Sophia appeared to buy into his narrative, prompting Earl to delve further into his perceived grievances. He alleged that Prince's seemingly innocent actions, such as leaving his favorite cup on the kitchen counter, were deliberate displays of asserting his dominance, along with leaving his favorite bowl in the sink.

I was in disbelief at the extent of Earl's fabrications. As Ms. Sophia called the twins into our session, I couldn't help but express my frustration. I reiterated my strong opposition to the twins moving out, which Earl was so adamant about. I emphasized their financial inability to sustain themselves independently. When questioned about their biological father, I reiterated again that they had severed ties with him long ago, since the age of 3, due to his inability to be a dad to them. Despite my efforts to redirect the conversation toward marriage counseling, Ms. Sophia allowed Earl to continue to monopolize the session with complaints about the twins and me.

After the session, we discussed our frustrations in the car. I learned that Ms. Sophia had inquired about the twins' readiness to move out and encouraged them to reconnect with their biological father despite my clear objections. Feeling disillusioned with Ms. Sophia's approach, I voiced my decision not to return to counseling, a sentiment echoed by Mona and

Prince. Earl remained silent, then faking agreement, but I knew his allegiance lay elsewhere. It was evident that Ms. Sophia's handling of the sessions had only exacerbated our family's discord rather than fostering resolution.

THE DISCARD: REASONS NARCISSISTIC PARENTS REPLACE THEIR CHILDREN (*Earl wanted to discard my kids just as he had already discarded his own.*)

Individuals with high levels of narcissism often encounter difficulties in forming emotionally healthy connections with others. Instead, they tend to gravitate towards individuals who can fulfill their needs with minimal effort on the narcissist's part. These individuals typically seek a steady stream of people who bolster their sense of importance and superiority.

Known as their "narcissistic supply," this support network often includes individuals who can be easily manipulated into condoning and participating in the narcissist's problematic behavior towards others and who are willing to tolerate mistreatment themselves. Children, due to the inherent power dynamics in the parent-child relationship, can become prime sources of readily available supply for narcissistic parents who seek to shape and control them according to their desires.

However, in some instances, children of narcissists may find themselves seemingly replaced by their parent's affection. This replacement often occurs with a child of similar age and gender, though it can also involve a different individual replicating certain aspects of the parent-child dynamic.

They Struggle with Intricate Relationships

Narcissists typically display emotional immaturity. When relationships grow more emotionally intricate, especially as a child matures from adolescence to adulthood, the narcissistic parent may perceive it as a threat. In response, they may find it simpler to substitute the emotionally intricate individual with someone easier to handle.

They Harbor Jealousy Toward the Child

Due to their profound insecurities, narcissists often experience intense jealousy towards others. This jealousy can sometimes extend to their children. If the parent perceives the child not as someone they can control and exploit but as someone who accentuates their shortcomings, they may associate with someone they perceive as less threatening.

They Seek to Maintain the Facade of Being a Good Parent

Narcissists prioritize appearances; for many, appearing as a commendable parent is integral to their self-image. If their child, for any reason, fails to enhance their image, the narcissistic parent may choose to replace them with someone who portrays them as a nurturing and exemplary individual.

They Seek to Inflict Pain Upon their Child

Narcissists lack empathy and are motivated by their self-gratification, often disregarding the impact on others. Their emotions are easily wounded, and due to their immaturity, they may struggle to communicate their hurt maturely, resorting to passive-aggressive behavior. Substituting their child with another individual is a deliberate tactic to cause harm, perhaps in retaliation for perceived slights from the child.

PSYCHOSIS

Madness, blindness, and confusion of heart

– Deuteronomy 28:28

Earl's erratic behavior shattered the peace of our quiet, manicured lawn, middle-class, gated community. The scene outside our home was chaotic, with a swarm of at least 7 police SUVs and two ambulances attending to Mona and Prince. Prince's injuries were severe, requiring emergency surgery in the trauma unit, while Mona was also rushed away for serious medical attention. I felt helpless as I watched my children being taken away separately, unable to be with either of them. The house became a crime scene, and I was barred from re-entering as forensic teams arrived to gather evidence.

While providing my testimony to one of the officers, I received news that Earl had been apprehended in the middle of an intersection with the lights off, just sitting there. Meanwhile, Alexis was recounting her version of events to a separate officer leading up to the stabbing, detailing a troubling conversation she had with Earl after I had left to distance myself from him.

According to Alexis, Earl, still seething with anger, made disturbing remarks about Prince, stating, *"I could do something really bad to him,"* a sentiment he repeated multiple times during their interaction. Despite Alexis's protests, Earl insisted on walking, and she reluctantly followed him out of the house next door to her home. Before leaving, Earl requested money from Alexis, claiming he didn't want to be without cash. She obliged, handing him one of her credit cards as she had no cash. Earl then left and remained absent for several hours.

As I concluded my testimony with the officer, I recounted the events that unfolded as I drove home later that night. While driving home, my phone notifications alerted me to activity on the garage camera. I watched in disbelief as Earl attempted to access Prince's Jeep. Immediately, I called Prince to inquire if he had given Earl the keys, receiving an irritated denial in response. I assured Prince that I would handle the situation. Upon arriving at the gated entrance, I spotted Earl on the other side, already exiting.

With rage evident in his bloodshot eyes and veins bulging from his bald head, Earl unleashed a barrage of insults.

"Where were you, you f***ing b***h?" he spat venomously. Taken aback, I retorted,

"You already know where I was."

Earl persisted, demanding an answer and hurling derogatory terms at me. Choosing not to engage further, I shook my head side to side and proceeded towards home, with Earl trailing closely behind.

As we both pulled into the driveway, I swiftly pushed the button to open the garage door and went through to the kitchen, then upstairs to the bedroom. Passing by the hallway, I could hear the twins laughing in Mona's room, immersed in the amusement of funny reels on Prince's phone as normal. I stuck my head in to let them know I was home, and then I retreated into my bedroom, bracing myself for the storm that would follow.

After a while, of what seemed to be about ten minutes, Earl came charging up the stairs, swiftly making his way down the hallway and into our room, hastily closing the door behind him. His expression was contorted with rage as he approached me, yelling, *"You got the kids laughing at me!!!"* while pulling my hair and pinning me down on the bed. With his left forearm pressing against the right side of my chin and his hand pressing down on mine, he exerted his body weight, attempting to force my face away from him. In his frenzy, I noticed him reaching for something on the right side of his hip.

Frantically kicking and squirming, I prevented him from obtaining whatever he was reaching for. Mona and Prince burst into the room, alarmed by the commotion.

"What did you do to her?" Prince cried out. Startled, Earl released me and lunged towards Prince. In one swift motion, he drew a large butcher knife from the right side of his shorts, taking his left arm, gripping Prince around the neck, and viciously stabbing him.

Earl thrust the knife into Prince's stomach multiple times, then slashed across his upper lip, the right side of his head, and his right shoulder. The attack also severed nerves in his left hand, leaving him with permanent weakness and loss of strength in his fingers. Despite Mona's frantic screams for Prince and her desperate efforts to pull him away, she couldn't stop Earl's relentless attack. In the struggle, she suffered severe stab wounds to her upper chest near the collarbone and forearm.

Meanwhile, I was on the other side, screaming, "NO!!! NO!!!" as I grasped at Earl's shirt, desperately trying to pull him away from my son. I fought with everything I had, clawing at his face in a frantic attempt to gouge his eyes, but his overpowering strength and sweat-slicked skin made it impossible—my fingers just slid across his eyelids. In the chaos, he slashed the top of my right foot, leaving a deep, searing laceration. Still gripping Prince tightly, Earl slammed him onto his back and continued to stab him in the stomach. Prince cried out in agony, pleading, "OH GOD, PLEASE STOP!!!"

Miraculously, Prince was released and fled down the hall and stairs. Earl briefly lost sight of him, checked Prince's bedroom *(where his bloody handprint was left on the light switch),* and then rushed down the stairs to continue his pursuit of Prince. Mona, following behind, collapsed on the landing, nearly losing consciousness. Meanwhile, I was in the bedroom, hysterically trying to unlock my cell phone, screaming to myself in fear and hysterics, "CALL THE COPS!!! CALL THE COPS!!!"

As I spoke with the police, I frantically moved back and forth, trying to explain the situation, giving the license plate number and type of vehicle while searching for my children, calling their names, and racing down the hallway toward the stairs. As provoked by my voice, Mona managed to get up and run through the garage. In shock, she called Prince to come to her, but he hesitated, fearing Earl might run him over.

Prince found refuge at Alexis' house, urgently calling her from her driveway, shouting up to her bedroom window, "Alexis, he stabbed me! Call the police!" Meanwhile, Earl got into my SUV, leaving behind a bloody trail.

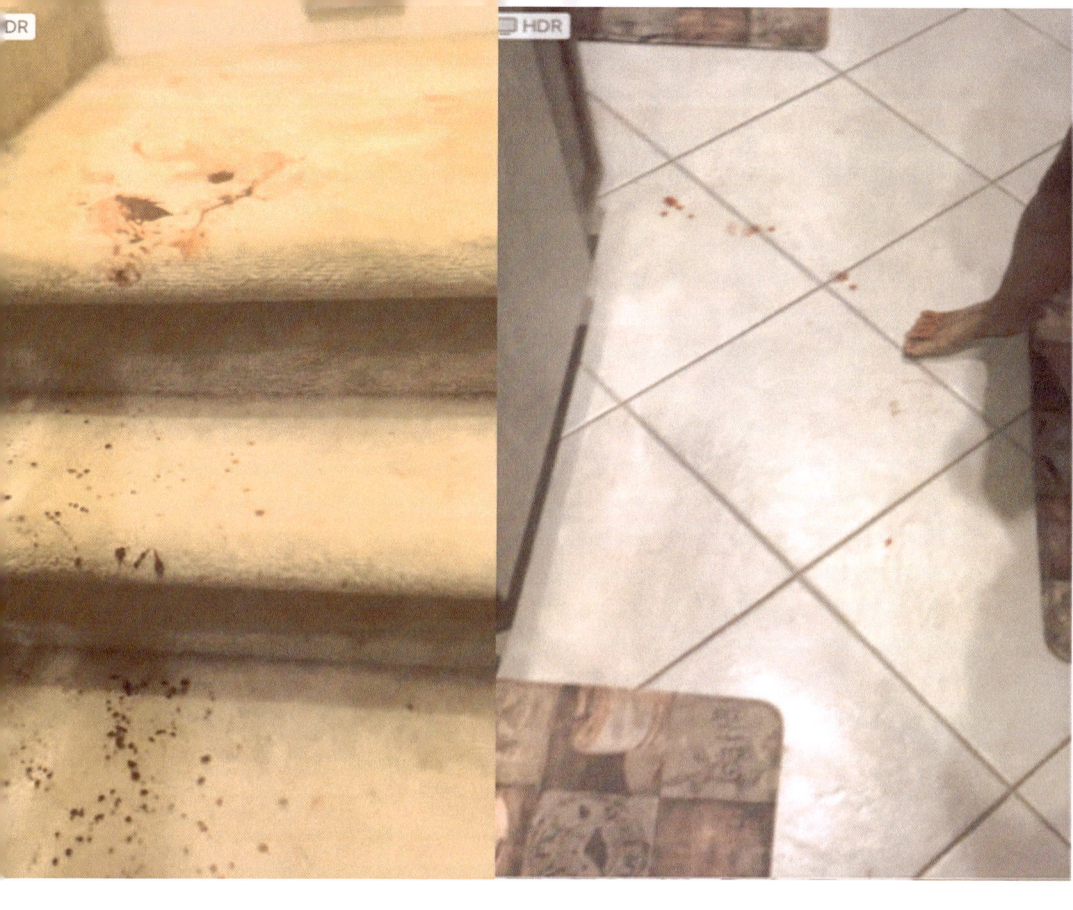

This is where Mona collapsed on the steps, drifting in and out of consciousness until she heard my voice calling her name. She had been stabbed three times—twice in the chest, near her neck and collarbone, and once in her forearm. Blood was pooling around her foot, a stark reminder of how much she was losing. Blood was everywhere spattered across the main bedroom, smeared along the hallway, walls, and doors, and trailing down to the kitchen floor, garage, and even into the driveway.

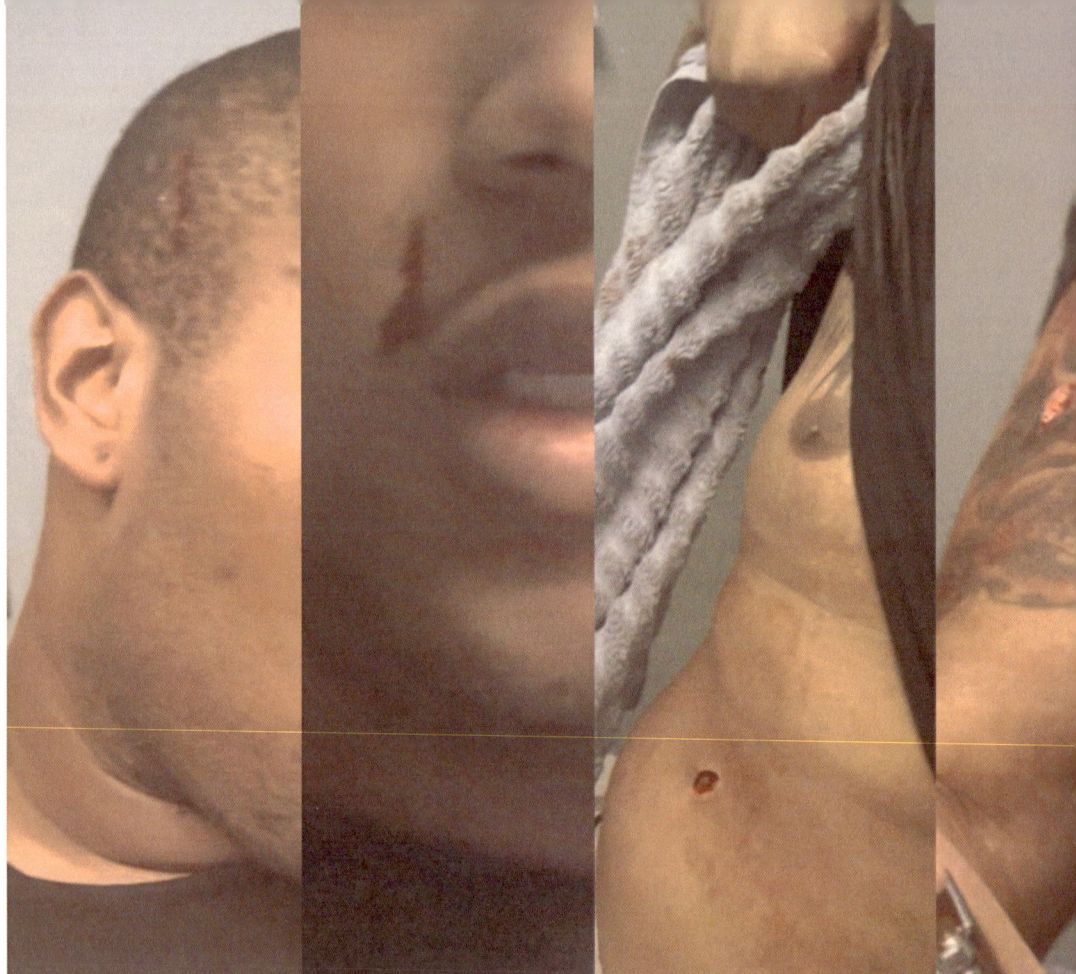

The photos show Prince's injuries from being stabbed a total of nine times—on the right side of his head, the top right of his lip, the left side of his stomach, and the right side of his shoulder. He also suffered deep lacerations along the creases inside his fingers. With every exhale, blood gushed from his stomach like a faucet. The next image reveals the sheer force behind the attack, as the knife used was bent nearly in half.

The white arrow highlights Prince in Alexis' driveway, standing by a tree and shouting for her to call the police, while Earl hurriedly gets into the SUV to flee the scene. Not long after, the police apprehended Earl, finding him parked in the middle of an intersection with the SUV's lights off. He was detained, and his bond was set at $25,003.

DEPOSITION/PREP/TRIAL

And you will know the truth, and the truth will set you free

– John 8:32

On February 1, 2024, the twins and I had to participate in a deposition with Earl's lawyer via Zoom alongside our prosecuting attorney and the court stenographer. Due to scheduling, we logged into the virtual meeting from our separate bedrooms on our personal computers. Earl's lawyer took over 30 minutes a piece, questioning each of us about the events leading up to the current situation and our testimonies.

When it was my turn to speak with his attorney, I detailed how Mona and Prince initially embraced Earl as their father, but their feelings shifted to resentment as he spiraled into heavy drinking, car destruction, and unfulfilled promises to stop drinking. I then recounted the events of the fateful night. (*Prince had come downstairs for a drink of water, wearing his headphones, endearingly touching my cheek with his nose before returning to his room without speaking to anyone because he had already interacted with everyone earlier that day, including Earl.*

Earl took offense to Prince's silence and began arguing with me, insisting that Prince acknowledge him. Despite explaining that Prince had already spoken to everyone earlier, Earl stormed up the stairs, banged on Prince's door, and assumed a confrontational posture, clapping his hands together in a threatening gesture. However, Prince remained inside his room, standing at his open door, refusing to engage with Earl, which only fueled Earl's anger. He demanded that I compel Prince to speak to him, but Prince refused, revealing that his courtesy towards Earl was solely for my sake and that he was tired of pretending.

This declaration further enraged Earl, who bypassed me and began pacing the kitchen in agitation. As I descended the stairs, I overheard Earl whispering to himself, muttering angrily. When I approached him, I suggested ending the discussion, but Earl confronted me aggressively in my face, accusing me of mocking him. I reassured him that his accusation was untrue. Still sensing the escalating tension, I decided to leave to do Instacart (something Earl and I did for fun for what we would call "house money" kept in a jar for junk food of pizza and snacks for rainy days), leaving out to do this was my way of avoiding further confrontation. Mona had already gone to work while Alexis remained behind, attempting to calm Earl down.

I shared that after we came home from the hospital that night, how difficult it was to return to a bloody crime scene throughout our home. It wasn't until later that Alexis and I did a thorough cleaning in both houses, as she had blood spills from her driveway into her living room, where she let Prince in.

Mona, Prince, and I were too afraid to sleep alone in our separate bedrooms, fearing Earl might return to finish what he started. The fear was so overwhelming that Mona and I chose to sleep in Prince's bed, locking his door every day and night for over a week. I held them close, one on each side of me, offering what little comfort I could in the midst of our terror.)

From the look on his lawyer's face, it was clear that I had revealed more than he expected. He shook his head from side to side disapprovingly, clearly disturbed by what he was hearing. He then asked if Earl had attempted to contact me. I detailed how Earl had mailed a written statement, supposedly written by Prince, requesting a change to his original testimony. In this false account, Earl wanted Prince to claim that he had stabbed himself, accidentally injured Mona and me, and punched Earl in the forehead, making Prince appear as the aggressor. This was a stark reversal from Earl's original claim that the kids and I had attacked him. Earl even asked me to have Prince sign this false document and submit it to the Clerk of Court.

The lawyer's disbelief was evident as he shook his head from side to side again. It was clear that Earl's actions violated the court's orders to avoid contacting us. He refused to take responsibility for his actions and instead attempted to blame the victims.

Shortly after our Zoom meeting with Earl's attorney, we learned that Earl had requested that his lawyer be removed from the case. His foolish attempt to represent himself in court had backfired, with the judge dismissing his efforts, calling them 'baseless.' Consequently, Earl's attorney was reassigned to him and has since submitted multiple requests for continuances, causing delays lasting nearly two years.

JUSTICE HAS BEEN SERVED

When justice is done, it brings joy to the righteous but terror to evildoers

– Proverbs 21:15

Months passed before we finally received an update from the prosecuting State Attorney, Mrs. Tyler. Earl's charges had been elevated to two counts of first-degree attempted murder—one for each of the twins—along with an additional charge of domestic battery stemming from domestic violence against me.

During this time, our legal team located Earl's ex-wife in South Carolina, who had survived a previous murder attempt by him. She was preparing to testify about her own harrowing experience alongside the police officers who had handled her case. Jury selection was scheduled for January 27, 2025. As the date drew closer, with the trial taking place on January 28, 2025, I found myself filled with conflicting emotions.

While there was relief in knowing the case was progressing, it was accompanied by a deep dread. The idea of facing him again, of being in the same room during the trial, made me long for a way to testify without ever having to see his face. Mona, Prince, and Alexis shared those same feelings.

On January 21, 2025, Prince, Alexis, and I went to Mrs. Tyler's office to prepare for the trial. Mrs. Tyler and her partner, Mrs. Julia walked us through the step-by-step process of what to expect in court. One by one, we were taken to a separate room to review our accounts of what had happened, essentially providing our statements.

Mona was flying in from Alaska, where she works as a Merchant Mariner on boats for the government in the engine room, following a schedule of two months at sea and one month at home. She was also due to arrive in a few days to undergo her trial preparation. Time was critical, as Prince was set to begin his journey as a soldier in the United States Army the following week.

January 28, 2025—the day of the trial. Around 4 PM, I was the first to be called to testify. After being sworn in, I took the witness stand. Mrs. Julia began by asking me my name, age, occupation, how long Earl and I had been married, and if he was present in the courtroom. I was then required to point him out and describe the color of his clothing.

This was incredibly difficult for me. I didn't want to look at him, but when I finally did, I saw that he was already staring at me with cold, unfriendly eyes—almost threatening.

Mrs. Julia instructed me to explain what happened on September 1, 2023, to the jurors. As I recounted the events, I couldn't stop the tears from falling, especially when the pictures from that night were displayed on the computer, along with the actual knife displayed inside a clear box case. Seeing those images and the knife was gut-wrenching, but speaking about them was even harder, particularly when describing how my children were attacked. The memories flooded back intensely as I struggled to put them into words.

When my attorney finished questioning me, the prosecuting attorney representing Earl's side began his cross-examination. His questions felt superficial, lacking substance or weight. It was clear he was grasping at straws. He attempted to trip me up by mentioning the car situation—specifically, which car Earl had driven off in that night. He claimed to be confused, suggesting I'd previously given conflicting statements. I firmly clarified that I had not and repeated my testimony accurately.

The prosecutor attempted to suggest that everyone in the house had been upset the morning of September 1, 2023. I firmly corrected him, clarifying that Earl was the only one who was upset and that he woke up in that state. Flustered, the prosecutor shuffled through his paperwork before stepping away and approaching Earl. He then asked the judge if he minded for a brief recess. With a sharp and resolute tone, the judge responded, "No, I do mind, and I'm wrapping this up."

After a tense pause, Earl's attorney returned to the podium, his voice steady but sharp as he stated he had no further questions. The room fell silent, the weight of the moment settling in. It was just after 4:30 PM, and the judge, with a final glance at the courtroom, adjourned until the next morning at 10 AM. The air felt thick with anticipation as Prince, Mona, and Alexis were set to testify the following day.

Through our team, Mrs. Tyler and Mrs. Collier, we learned that Earl's ex-wife, Tonya, had been placed on standby at a hotel, ready to testify if needed. The courts had allowed our side to bring up his past, and they were prepared to call her in should Earl decide to take the stand. What we discovered next shook me to my core. Everything Earl had ever told me about his ex-wife was a lie. He lied about her name and painted her as a monster, but according to our attorneys, Tonya is a sweet, Christian woman who was working as a nursing consultant. Because of the horrors Earl had inflicted on her, she would never be able to work again.

He had stabbed her over 30 times, leaving scars that would never heal—physically, mentally, or emotionally. The brutality of his actions had left her unable to walk without a cane, struggling with urinary incontinence, and haunted by PTSD. Given the sensitive nature of the case, I had yet to meet her, but my heart broke for everything she had endured. I pray every day that God continues to watch over her. I wish I could wrap her in a hug and apologize for what she had to suffer at the hands of a "monster"—the very word she used to describe him, a description that still lingers in my mind.

On January 28, 2025, the courtroom was charged with energy as Prince, Mona, and Alexis were called individually to the stand. The defense attorneys tried, and failed, to trip them up with conflicting questions. With unwavering resolve, they stood their ground, repeating exactly what they had stated two years ago, undeterred by the pressure.

The drama peaked on January 29, 2025—closing arguments day. The twins chose to stay home, leaving Alexis and me to face the day. We vowed we wouldn't leave until a verdict was delivered, whether it took five hours or kept us in that courtroom until 9 PM. Our attorneys delivered powerful, impassioned closings, presenting hard facts to the jurors with unshakable intensity. Our victim's advocate, Mrs. Collier was a constant presence by our side, walking us through every legal term and ensuring we understood each moment's significance. An incredible team surrounded us, and I will forever be grateful for their support.

We waited a couple of hours for the jury to come up with a verdict. They deliberated from 3:17 PM to 5:51 PM. They found Earl guilty of a lesser included offense of attempted murder in the second degree with a weapon on Prince, then guilty a second time of a lesser included offense of attempted manslaughter by act with a weapon on Mona, and then guilty of battery (domestic) on me. They labeled Earl as a habitual felony offender, prison release re-offender, and habitual violent felony offender. The entire three days were quite intense.

The sentencing was set for 11 AM on March 3, 2025. Prince couldn't be there—he was already in boot camp. Mona had returned from Alaska, but didn't want to attend with Alexis and me, but offered moral support in spirit.

Full of anxiety, we sat down with Mrs. Tyler, one of our attorneys, who would be presenting only Mona's statement. Prince's statement wouldn't be read, not because it lacked importance, but because it didn't fully convey how the incident had impacted him. He had never wanted to write one, and it was clear in his words—or rather, the lack of them. Writing those impact statements was something none of us were ready for. We had already found a quiet sense of peace, knowing Earl had been found guilty, confident he would face a long sentence. But our attorneys insisted. They explained that the judge needed to hear how this ordeal had shattered our lives. It would help guide the judges' decision per our attorney. Reluctantly, we complied.

As we walked into the courtroom, Earl immediately had continuous glares, looking back at us with cold, big black eyeballs as if he were just a shell of a body and something else staring us down. I felt nothing from his being. No connection, no history. One of the bailiffs caught wind of his stares and stood in between our view so that when Earl would look back again, he would see the bailiff. Noticing that we were no longer within his sight, he suddenly shouted, "I DIDN'T STAB NOBODY!!!" (*It seemed he had conveniently forgotten the apologies he gave to Prince and Mona for stabbing them— admissions he made during his first and second calls from jail, which were recorded. But we hadn't forgotten. We also recorded those calls on video from one of our phones, every word preserved as evidence.*)

After a brief silence, he yelled again, "THAT'S A LIE!!!" From that point, Earl's behavior took a darker turn. He erupted into belligerent outbursts—shouting at Judge Saunders and even directing his fury toward his own attorney. His arrogance was on full display as he exchanged words with the judge, ignoring multiple warnings to remain silent. The atmosphere in the courtroom became thick with tension, and the situation quickly spiraled out of control.

Three bailiffs, moving swiftly, began walking toward him, clearly ready to intervene. At that point, Judge Saunders had to remind Earl of the previous reprimands from the bailiffs. With unflinching authority, the judge warned Earl that he would be removed from the courtroom and sentencing would continue without him if he dared to utter another outburst. The room seemed to hold its breath, waiting for Earl to either comply or test the judge's patience further.

With the room being under control for the moment, Mrs. Tyler and Earl's attorney discussed with Judge Saunders whether Earl's past could be introduced, showing him to be a habitual re-offender. After less than a second thought, Judge

Saunders granted permission. My attorney then informed the judge that a few victim impact statements were to be read. My heart was hammering in my chest, each beat reverberating in my ears. This was the moment we would face the full weight of everything. I had decided to go first, with Mrs. Tyler reading Mona's statement afterward.

During my reading, Earl tested the judge's patience. He couldn't contain himself. As I tried to read my victim impact statement, his disruptive voice cut through every word. "WHAT?!!" "ARE YOU SERIOUS?!!" "YOU'RE A LIAR!!" His mocking tone followed with a loud, "YEAH, OKAY, MMHMPH!!" The judge's patience snapped, and he ordered the bailiffs to remove Earl from the courtroom. With Earl finally out, I finished my statement in the tense silence. Then, Mrs. Tyler stepped up to read Mona's statement, the weight of it all lingering in the air.

My victim impact statement: *I never imagined standing in court in front of a judge to speak about a trial of this nature that involves me and my children. How a person that I grew up with and known all my life that I loved and trusted could turn my life and the lives of my kids into a nightmare. We were family and the bond we shared, gave me a sense of comfort, as though I was safe in Earl's care, but that illusion was shattered when he tried to take me and my kids lives—the lives of his own family. I still remember the fear I felt as Earl turned against us in the most violent way. A feeling of betrayal that I can't shake. "A plant."*
(I chose the word "plant" deliberately, knowing Earl would understand its meaning. It was a term he and I used pertaining to certain family members who pretended to be friendly with us, but in reality, were acting as spies, feeding information and causing us harm - monitoring spirits) *The terror of knowing that he could take away not only my life but the lives of my kids is a pain I can't fully express. My kids saved my life when they walked in on him abusing me. Earl managed to stab me on the foot but what he did to my kids is what makes him a monster.*

Earl stabbed my daughter 3x and my son 9x and chased after him to finish the job. As a mother, my first instinct is to protect my kids, yet in that moment, I felt powerless, like we were trapped in a horror we couldn't escape.

Since that day, for a week straight, my kids and I have slept in the same bed together with the door locked feeling like he was going to come down the hallway to get us. We felt so unsafe in our own home. We wouldn't go to any part of the house unless we were all together and that included going to the bathroom or going to the kitchen to hurry to grab food and run back to the room to lock the door. I hate reading this because we have to relive it…We trusted Earl, and he turned that trust into fear. Every day, I wonder why someone who promised to love and protect us could be capable of such cruelty. It's just evil and demonic. "A plant."

As a Christian, God says I have to forgive him, but the vision of it all and the scars are something we will carry forever, especially my kids. I pray for healing—for them, and myself, but I also pray for justice. We deserve to feel safe, to be able to finally move forward knowing that Earl cannot hurt or try to kill us again. Since this all happened, I find myself not wanting to leave the house unless I absolutely have to. I don't even want to be here because I always have a feeling of pressure from him in my head like I need to hurry back home. Even making trips to the grocery store makes me paranoid because I look at everyone side-eyed, thinking they know what happened. I don't trust anyone and think people are up to something. I had to force myself to sleep in my own bedroom again because the vision of the whole incident wouldn't leave my mind. Keeping the lights on throughout the house became a solution. I had many sleepless nights staying up, checking on my twin's wounds, and making sure they were still breathing. I couldn't protect them then, and it angers me so much because God blessed me with them and trusted me to be their mom, and I failed at protecting them because I trusted him.

I hope the court will understand the depth of the pain Earl caused and will ensure that he is held accountable for his actions, even if he doesn't feel like he has anything to be accountable for by having the audacity to plead not guilty then lie to say it was my son who did it all. We cannot rewrite what happened, but we can seek justice for the future that was almost snatched away from us. Earl tried to end my and my kid's lives, but God said no. And now, He is going to show Earl exactly who God is.

Mona's victim impact statement: *After the incident on September 1st, I suffered a stab wound on my right forearm that needed stitches and two gashes on my chest. When we came home from the hospital, we all slept in my brother's room. We were afraid to sleep with the lights off or the door opened. We were afraid that Earl would somehow find his way back to us to finish the job. I had to leave work for several days. When I thought I was ready to go back, it was too soon as I was too worried for my mom and brother, and I ended up leaving work early. My mother was working two jobs to keep us afloat. When Earl finally had a job, his income was helping keep up the house so Mom could let one go.*

After the incident, I ended up selling my motorcycle and getting a better paying job to help with household bills. I had to give up my kitten because I couldn't afford to take care of him. Our carpet was stained in blood, so we had to tear it up. We walked on bare floorboard for nearly a year. When we were finally ready to sleep in our own rooms, I was up for several nights, listening and staying awake in case I had to be prepared for an emergency. I suffered nightmares of Earl returning and had to distract myself from thinking about the situation. I still suffer nightmares and can never fully relax or sleep at night. I refuse to sleep with earbuds like I used to in case of an emergency.

Mentally, I've been traumatized and scarred. I find myself becoming quickly angered and irritable. Sometimes getting crying spells, and random waves of sadness or depression, and avoiding men that resemble Earl or remind me of him. I'm self-conscious about my scars and overall embarrassed by this whole situation. I would like for Earl to stay in prison. He contributes nothing to society, and I don't want to see him ever. Earl would have killed my mom; he nearly killed my brother. I feel like the prison will and should be his new home.

Even though Prince's victim impact statement wasn't read aloud in court, I've included it in this book. I felt it was important—his voice deserved to be heard, and his words had to be part of this story.

Prince's victim impact statement: *The incident impacted my body, I have 4 wounds that itch frequently on my stomach, right shoulder, the side of my head, and my upper lip. Mentally, the situation impacted how I look at people with knives in their hands. If I see anyone holding a knife, I now think of what's the best way to maneuver the knife away from me if they come at me. Which could potentially be an issue in the army with me being a culinary specialist.*

With the court proceeding in Earl's absence, his attorney arranged for his daughter and mother to attend via Zoom to speak on his behalf, hoping to share something positive about Earl in an effort to prevent a harsh sentence. Shaniqua, Earl's daughter, was the first to speak. She began by recounting the same story I shared at the beginning of this book about how our paths crossed. She explained how I came across her Instagram page, saw Earl's picture, and we connected. I introduced myself and explained how we were related.

She was mostly truthful, but things took a turn when she said, "After my dad moved to Florida with 'her,' we didn't have contact with him anymore because she sent me a text saying none of his kids should reach out to him." She even went so far as to claim she could prove it, knowing full well that the court wasn't likely to ask for evidence during sentencing.

The truth is, when I reached out to Shaniqua on social media to ask about Earl, we never exchanged phone numbers—not once. To this day, I don't even know her phone number, though she might have mine since I'm a counselor and a business owner, and my contact information is easily found online. We had some great conversations through Instagram Messenger, but that was as far as it went. It all came to an abrupt end when Aunt Karen ordered Shaniqua to stop talking to me and she then blocked me. Alexis suspects that Shaniqua may have fabricated parts of her story—possibly even doctoring our messages and photoshopping my number into conversations. While I can't be certain, I'd love to see what kind of so-called "evidence" she claims to have.

Shaniqua then reminisced about her 'close' relationship with her father, recalling how Earl once took her shopping for college clothes. She conveniently omitted that this happened over 15 years ago when she was just a teenager. Now, in her mid-30s, her story sounded like a distant memory. Oddly enough, her account mirrored a story Earl once told me—(*He realized that Shaniqua had deceived him at her mother's insistence, manipulating him into buying clothes for her half-sister. Shaniqua had requested smaller-sized outfits under the pretense that they were for herself, only for him to later discover they were actually intended for the other child.*)

Shaniqua then brought up how she learned about Earl and me getting married—during a one-time visit to see him in prison while he was serving time for attempted murder. She claimed she wanted to introduce her then-husband to Earl. (*Per Earl, she only came to visit because they were on their way out of town to go clubbing with friends, and his location was along the route.*) At this point, Mrs. Tyler began cross-examining her, challenging the supposed closeness between her and Earl. She cut straight to the truth: "The reality is, your father chose to cut off contact with you and his other children." Shaniqua, visibly unsettled, quickly shot back: "I have a text from 'her.'" Mrs. Tyler didn't hesitate. "Well, do you have proof of who was on the other end of that text?" The question hit hard, leaving Shaniqua silent.

In reality, Earl's own children—especially his sons—wanted nothing to do with him. During the time of spending 10 years in prison for attempting to murder Tonya, none of his children, parents, or siblings ever visited him, according to Earl. (*He confided in me that Aunt Karen resented me for being the one who visited him every weekend for three years, right up until COVID-19 restrictions hit—while she never once made the effort in spite of her many trips to visit friends and his location was along the route*) Out of six sons, only two reached out after his release, and both explicitly stated they wanted no part in his life. I was present during those calls. One son had been murdered due to his involvement in a dangerous lifestyle, and another was serving a good number of years in prison for drug and gang-related charges. Shaniqua continued her claims, insisting that she had messages where I allegedly told her and her siblings not to contact him. The judge abruptly cut in before she could go further: "Yeah, I think I understand." With that, she was dismissed. Mrs. Tyler had no further questions.

Now, it was Aunt Karen's turn to speak on Earl's behalf. Instead of offering anything positive, she immediately launched into victim-blaming, just as Shaniqua had. Earl's attorney reminded her, just as he had reminded Shaniqua, that they were there to advocate for leniency in Earl's sentencing—not to attack the victims, but Aunt Karen couldn't help herself. Her voice was laced with anger as she claimed that my tears over my children being stabbed while reading my victim impact statement were nothing more than an act—that I was, in her words, "quite the actress." She went on, insisting that I had no business contacting Earl in the first place, insinuating that none of this would have happened if I had never contacted Shaniqua. Her hatred for me was palpable.

She then accused me of having ulterior motives, claiming my entire relationship with Earl was driven by revenge— though she never clarified against whom or why. She only continued her veiled attacks, stating that she had so much more to say but had been instructed not to by Earl's attorney. Then, she turned on the court. She lashed out at Earl's own lawyer, claiming that he, Mrs. Tyler, and even Judge Saunders were no different from prosecutors—stating her son was denied a fair trial. She reminded Earl's attorney that she had told him this when they spoke the week before.

She went on to say that, as a mother, she could never condone children getting hurt, and she uttered, insincerely, *I hope 'they' are okay*, no mention of me. However, in the same breath, she added that no one truly knows what happened, especially if Earl was defending himself. She questioned whether anyone really knew the truth, pointing out that there were no cameras inside the house where the incident occurred—only footage from the outside cameras showing Earl leaving the scene of the crime.

Not long after, she tried to justify Earl's actions, claiming that he wasn't a narcissist but rather a victim of childhood trauma. She went on to reveal that Earl had experienced something traumatic when he was around 10 years old, something he shared with her less than five years ago. What Earl shared was that he had been molested by his uncle—Aunt Karen's brother. According to her, he needed psychiatric evaluation, never prison. Earl's attorney interrupted, firmly reminding her that this was not Earl's first time in prison—that he had previously served time for attempted murder on his first wife and that the judge had to have him removed from the courtroom due to his disrespectful outburst and behavior. Aunt

Karen had no response to that. Instead, she shifted her anger right back at me. (*A few weeks before this incident, while reminiscing about our past, Earl made a chilling confession—Dorothy, whom I had known from family gatherings, wasn't just an old flame. She was his first wife and the mother of five of his children. Then, he admitted something even more disturbing. During an argument, he accused her of cheating and, in a fit of rage, sliced the top of her lip. For years, I had assumed the scar was from a cleft lip. I never imagined it was a permanent mark left by his violence.*)

Neither Aunt Karen nor Shaniqua defended Earl well, and his disruptive behavior in court certainly didn't help his case. They only revealed their narcissistic responses by victim blaming and making excuses for Earl, along with lies and ignorance, and the court saw right through it. To top it off, Aunt Karen had the nerve to say, "God sees all and knows all." Before she could go any further, the judge cut her off and turned to Mrs. Tyler. "Do you have any questions for Ms. Baldwin?" the judge asked. Without even glancing at the screen to acknowledge Aunt Karen, Mrs. Tyler simply declined, her expression laced with disgust.

With that, Judge Saunders prepared to deliver Earl's sentence—until he realized that the Pre-Sentence Investigation (PSI) report had not yet arrived. He had ordered the PSI months prior but couldn't proceed with sentencing without it. The judge immediately ordered a rush request, marking it STAT, and rescheduled the sentencing for March 12, 2025, at 1:30 PM. Mona decided she wouldn't attend, but Alexis and I made plans to be there.

The Final Verdict

Alexis and I arrived at the courthouse twenty minutes before sentencing. We met with Mrs. Collier, who escorted us inside, where Mrs. Tyler was already waiting. This was it—the finale. I half-expected Aunt Karen and Shaniqua to appear on Zoom in support of Earl, but they didn't show. Not for him. Not for this moment.

Then, the bailiffs escorted Earl in. For a brief second, our eyes met—but he quickly looked away. Judge Saunders turned to Earl's attorney and Mrs. Tyler, asking if they had any final statements before sentencing. His attorney declined, but Mrs. Tyler pressed forward, reminding the court that Earl was a repeat offender who had committed this crime while on parole. The judge allowed it.

Then, Earl was given the chance to speak on his own behalf—to show remorse. Instead, he did the opposite. He pulled out four pages, densely packed with lies, fumbling as he tried to present them as truth. His timeline was a mess—dates and years were completely wrong. His claims were even more absurd. He said I had been homeless with my children, coming to his prison cell to beg him for help. He accused me of using him to improve his credit score, to buy a home, and to fund my so-called fraudulent businesses—businesses I had built from the ground up for over 15 years and are still thriving.

The courtroom fell into stunned silence. The judge. The bailiffs. Even Earl's own attorney. Every expression was the same—disbelief. Then, before launching into his tirade about me being a "fraud," he tried to suggest that he and the judge had a private conversation—one where the judge supposedly gave him permission to "share his side of the story."

Judge Saunders immediately shut that down. "We never had a private conversation," he said firmly, reminding Earl that the last time he was granted the opportunity to speak, he had to be removed for being disruptive. Cornered, Earl, backpedaled, quickly shifting to another web of delusions. He claimed that Prince's blood was fake, that he had splattered it around the house as part of a staged attack—insisting that Prince had stabbed himself nine times, Mona, three times, and then roughed Earl up to make it look like an assault.

When Prince ran next door to Alexis' house, desperately pleading for her to call the police, his blood trailed across the driveway and pooled on her living room floor. Yet, Earl insisted it was all fabricated, nothing more than an elaborate setup. He then alleged that someone had doctored the Ring footage, somehow splicing together clips from two separate days to frame him. As if that weren't enough, he claimed I had tricked him into marriage, convincing him to change my last name and the kids' last names—all because, according to him, I was committing fraud, and we needed new identities.

When his delusions failed to gain traction, he turned on his own attorney, insisting he had been misrepresented, and accused the judge of denying him a fair trial. He even went so far as to claim that the forensic team had botched their investigation. It was beyond ridiculous. He rambled for twenty, maybe twenty-five minutes until Judge Saunders had enough.

As I sat there listening, I couldn't stop thinking—What happened to him? Who was this person? Because this wasn't the Earl I once knew. This wasn't the family I grew up with. And then, the moment we had been waiting for. Judge Saunders read Earl's charges and then brought the gavel down with finality.

Attempted Murder in the Second Degree with a Weapon – Count 1: Life for Prince.

Attempted Manslaughter by Act with a Weapon – Count 2: 30 years for Mona.

Battery Domestic – Count 3: 365 days for me.

Life, plus 30 years.

Earl didn't flinch—his face was void of emotion as if he had already made peace with his fate. The bailiffs stepped forward, locking cuffs around his wrists and ankles, then escorted him out of the courtroom—out of our lives. After two long years, it was finally over. He would first be sent back to South Carolina to complete his remaining parole, face the violation charges from this case, and only then be returned to Florida to serve the life sentence he had just received.

(It had been over 20 years since I last saw Earl before our reunion nearly eight years ago, but never, even in my worst nightmares, did I imagine he would become the being he is today. He has transformed into a threat, not just to society but to himself. He was never mentally or emotionally prepared to be released from prison. Justice may have been served with a life sentence, but there are no true victories here. Mona, Prince, and Tonya will carry the scars of this nightmare forever, while Earl lost his soul long before that fateful day.

He ceased to be the Earl I once knew—the family I grew up with—and became something unrecognizable as if a dark force had consumed him over the years. My mind had been clouded by memories of who he once was, blinding me to the reality of what he had become.)

What Causes Narcissism?

The cause is likely complex. Narcissistic personality disorder may be linked to Environment — parent-child relationships with either too much adoration or too much criticism that doesn't match the child's actual experiences and achievements—Genetics — inherited characteristics, such as certain personality traits.

How Does Narcissism Develop?

Social learning theory holds that children are likely to grow up to be narcissistic when their parents overvalue them: when their parents see them as more special and more entitled than other children.

Narcissism ran deep within Earl's family, renowned in the community as the esteemed "Baldwins," considered untouchable in society. Their family name was highly regarded and cherished as one of their most valuable possessions. While some families may take pride in their lineage, the Baldwins took it to another level, aspiring to maintain their esteemed reputation at any cost.

However, behind their facade of respectability lay a dark truth unbeknownst to the public. Earl often emphasized the need to "live up to the family name," instilling narcissistic tendencies from an early age. This pressure to uphold their status created a sense of entitlement and arrogance among them, fostering a belief that they were above reproach. (*Aunt Karen ruled with an iron fist, her temper quick and unforgiving. She was always "hitting Earl upside the head" as if punishing him eased her own demons. It didn't matter whether we were at our house, her house, or our grandmother's—her aggression followed. My mother never hesitated to step in, her voice sharp with disapproval.*

"KAREN!" she yelled.
"WHAT?!" Aunt Karen snapped back.
"Stop hitting that boy like that!" my mother pleaded.
"He's getting on my damn nerves!" Aunt Karen shot back without a second thought.
"Well, don't do it in front of me!" my mother demanded, as if simply looking away could spare Earl from the abuse.

Earl was the second oldest of five, yet I only ever witnessed him, and Felecia take the blows. Felecia's moment came over her own leather jacket. Aunt Karen wanted to wear it—Felecia didn't want her to. That was enough. As they came down the stairs, Aunt Karen caught a look on Felecia's face that she didn't like. Without warning, she slammed her against the wall, her forearm pressing hard against Felecia's neck. Aunt Karen spat out a few choice words, then walked out the door—wearing the jacket she had just stolen with force.)

Earl's sister, Felecia, exemplified this narcissistic behavior despite her prominent position as a Judge. Behind closed doors, she was known for her manipulative and vindictive nature, earning more disdain than respect for her numerous instances of misconduct during her tenure as a Judge, which led to her suspension. She had a history of violence that came to light when she had dismissed charges of shooting her ex-husband, claiming self-defense when she invited him over to her home to "help move furniture," all while having an active restraining order on him that she would often remove and replace. As of recent, she was culminating in a charge of attempted murder after shooting her ex-boyfriend in the head while he slept, leaving him blind in one eye.

Despite the overwhelming evidence against her of the gun being registered in her name along with gun residue on her hands, Felecia refused to accept responsibility, shifting the blame onto the victim, insinuating that he shot himself while asleep. She is currently awaiting a trial set for April 7, 2025.

Unbeknownst to me at the time, Earl had a dark and violent history. Consumed by jealousy and rage, he had come dangerously close to killing his ex-wife in a violent stabbing fueled by accusations of infidelity. Like his sister, he evaded accountability, blaming his actions on the victims. Both Earl and Felecia followed a disturbing pattern of violence, with Earl's preferred method being stabbing, while Felecia resorted to shooting.

Such behavior is often rooted in familial patterns, with narcissistic personality disorder (NPD) perpetuated through generations. NPD families operate in a hierarchical manner, with the most dominant member at the helm, dictating the family's reality and suppressing dissent. In such environments, accountability is often elusive, as the blame is shifted onto the victims, perpetuating a cycle of abuse and manipulation.

Here is an example of the dynamics within a narcissistic family

Example of Family Dynamic with Narcissistic Personality Disorder

Pictures of NPD families are very diverse and may differ from this example

Mother with Covert NPD

Idealises the father and 'Golden' Child.

Father with Grandiose NPD

Idealises the self.

Sibling

'Scapegoat' Child

Is devalued.

Holds the negative feelings of the family and is seen as the cause of all the difficulties.

Can develop Schizoid or Borderline traits (or Personality Disorders), Complex PTSD, chronic people pleasing or co-dependency.

Will also develop an impaired real self and therefore live in an adapted self. There will be a split in the personality structure (structural dissociation).

NPD Child

'Golden' Child

Is idealised.

Identifies/allies with Mother (to identify with the father would threaten the father's position).

The child must be perfect for the mother.

(NPD is established by Age 3)

The Real Self is not accepted by the parents or the child and there is a spilt in the personality.

Characteristics of Family Members

There are no 'Whole Object Relations' - this means that a person cannot hold in mind simultaneously that people can be both good and bad. This is known as black and white thinking; "I am all good" or "I am all bad" and other people are "all good" or "all bad."

A lack of 'whole object relations' means that a person does not form a realistic and stable perception of others.

There is a lack of 'Object Constancy' - this means that when a person is hurt by or angry with someone, they cannot keep in mind that they like or love that person.

Impaired Self

Parent projects onto the child the unwanted aspects of themselves i.e., helplessness and hopelessness.

When child tries to activate its own real self, it will be attacked by the parents. It develops an impaired self which holds the feelings of badness, incompetence, shame, weakness, and the feeling of falling apart. These feelings will be repressed/acted out/or the child projects them onto others and coerces them into containing and processing them.

Narcissistic Adapted Self

Child defends against an 'Abandonment Depression' (and is dependent upon narcissistic supplies to defend against this) by constructing a grandiose false/adapted self.

The child will be supported and admired for giving up its real self.

Can only have relationships which are based on being able to maintain their narcissistic defences.

Child mirrors the perfect narcissistic adapted self of the parents back to the parents.

Dealing With a Covert Narcissist

It can be challenging to manage if you suspect someone in your life is a covert narcissist.

The person with narcissism could be a parent or other family member, a friend, a co-worker, or a romantic partner.

Although you may not be able to control the narcissist's actions in your life, you can control how to deal with and communicate with them so that you are not negatively affected by their actions.

What is most important when dealing with a covert narcissist is to keep yourself safe, not to provoke them or do anything that could put you in a vulnerable position.

Stay Calm

It can be difficult not to feel upset when you know a covert narcissist is manipulating you.

However, it is essential to remember that their actions are nothing personal against you and instead reflect their insecurities and deep-rooted issues.

Try not to react if they attempt to start a fight or gaslight you. Narcissists want you to take their attacks personally and want a reaction to maintain power over you. If this reaction is taken away, they may eventually realize they cannot hold leverage over you.

The Grey Rock Method

This is a technique where you deliberately act disengaged so that a narcissist loses interest in you.

The more you give attention to a narcissist (e.g., arguing with them), the more they thrive. Grey rock means that you cut off that supply the narcissists want.

"Grey rock is an incredibly unsettling experience for them (narcissists). Many people believe that to overpower a narcissist, you should call them out on their stuff, you should call them names, and you should fight as hard and as dirty as them. Nothing could be farther from the truth."

Dr. Ramani, Clinical Psychologist

Healthy Communication

It can be helpful to point out to a narcissist when they have done something rude or unkind. This should be done delicately so as not to expect a backlash of aggression.

You could attempt to convey empathy when appropriate and gently point out when they have done something rude or arrogant.

Likewise, you can praise them if they display healthy behaviors and acknowledge when they are disappointed about something. If the narcissist does not realize their behaviors are causing problems, they will be less motivated to seek help. Even if they do not want to seek help or see the problem with their actions, being called out could cause them to self-regulate their behavior in your presence.

Create A Healthy Distance

Depending on who the covert narcissist is, it can make it difficult to separate yourself from them. However, it can be essential to have some distance if the opportunity presents itself.

For instance, if the narcissist is a work colleague, you could request that you work in a different location from them. If the narcissist is a parent whom you live with, you could spend the night at a friend's house for some space.

If the narcissist is someone who you do not have to see regularly or at all, you can try to limit interactions with them as much as possible or cut off all contact in a safe way.

When dealing with a covert narcissist, it is also important not to behave in a way that can create more tension, making the situation worse.

For instance, it could be more helpful not to argue or confront the individual, expect them to see your point of view, or expect meaningful communication.

There may be many pushbacks expected from the narcissists, as well as them being upset that they are not getting what they want.

However, it is essential to remember that it is not your job to control that person's emotions; you can only control how you deal with them.

Maintain Healthy Boundaries

As covert narcissists have no issue with exploiting others, they do not have healthy boundaries. Thus, the people in their lives need to set limits for them.

Boundaries are a good way of letting people know your values and that you are conveying to the narcissist that their tactics are not working.

It may be helpful to remind yourself of why you have set boundaries so that you can keep focused when a narcissist attempts to cross those boundaries.

"Evaluate the relationship and boundaries: is this a relationship for you to continue? Is this a hurtful relationship?"

Dr. Daniel Fox, Licensed Psychologist

Create a Support System

When dealing with someone who has covert narcissism, it is essential to have a support system outside of the relationship.

As narcissists may emotionally manipulate and cause confusion, it is helpful to talk things through with people outside of the relationship who can give a more realistic insight into what the truth is.

This can help with any self-doubt you may have due to being manipulated.

Educate Yourself

Educating yourself on NPD can help you understand the covert narcissists' strengths and weaknesses so you can learn to manage the relationship better.

You can learn to understand the goals of covert narcissists so you can notice the tactics they are using to achieve this goal from you (e.g., such as maintaining control) and ensure they are not using you as a power source.

'Research about abuse and narcissism helped me learn that this situation would never change. When you realize and educate yourself, you start to accept the situation for what it is and learn the only way to be happy is to leave.'

'Georgia,' 32

AFTERWORD

I can't even begin to describe the emotional turmoil of this journey, the pain, the uncertainty, the constant battle with myself to stay strong. And now, after everything we've endured, we're finally here. The moment that would bring it all to a head. The final chapter of a nightmare that has felt never-ending. I drowned in a sea of anxiety and tangled emotions; each one crashed over me like a relentless wave.

My heart was heavy, weighed down by a sense of sadness that wrapped around me like a suffocating fog. Sadness for my children, who had to bear so much. Sadness for Tonya, whose life is now irreparably altered. Sadness for Earl, whose choices have left him in a life he never imagined. And then, there's the sadness for me—the quiet grief that I've barely allowed myself to feel.

I lost my mother the year before, but I haven't had the chance to properly mourn her. The grief was swallowed whole by this painful, two-year battle that now has finally ended. In the process, I lost a life partner, my family, and the innocence of my childhood memories with him that will never be the same. Sometimes, I wish I could erase it all from my mind.

In an attempt to fill the void, I've thrown myself into redecorating my home, as though rearranging my surroundings could somehow reset the chaos inside. I've replaced furniture three times over the last two years, completely remodeled, and ripped out all the blood-stained carpet, replacing it with hardwood flooring to match the rest of the house. Each change felt like a desperate attempt to start fresh, to create something new amidst the ruins.

I suddenly found solace in Christian yoga. At first, it was just an experiment, but it quickly became my refuge. The gentle stretches and the scripture-filled meditations quieted my racing thoughts and drew me even more close to God. In those moments of stillness, I found peace. And through helping others—counseling those in need—I've found a new sense of purpose, a reason to keep going, to rise above the pain. It's as if serving others allows me to breathe again, to reclaim a piece of myself that was lost in the storm.

Elva Chase, BCCC, is a Board-Certified Christian Counselor passionate about positively impacting individuals' lives. Born and raised in Harrisburg, Pennsylvania, she has dedicated herself to addressing domestic violence and homelessness issues as the Founder and President of Precious Hearts Foundation, a 501c3 nonprofit organization, domestic violence agency.

In addition to her work in counseling and advocacy, Elva is the Owner and Publisher of Esquire Publications, a global book publishing firm. Her commitment to promoting well-being extends to her current studies in Florida for a Ph.D. in Clinical Psychology.

Elva's profound interest in narcissism stems from her personal experiences within a marriage, driving her to explore and understand this complex topic. Through her diverse roles and endeavors, Elva continues contributing to the well-being of individuals and communities.

www.PreciousHeartsFoundation.org
www.EsquirePublications.com
www.ElvaChase.com

BIBLIOGRAPHY

Ahern, K. (2018). Institutional betrayal and gaslighting. *The Journal of perinatal & neonatal nursing, 32*(1), 59-65.

Baskin-Sommers, A., Krusemark, E., & Ronningstam, E. (2014). Empathy in narcissistic personality disorder: from clinical and empirical perspectives. Personality Disorders: Theory, Research, and Treatment, 5(3), 323.

Brummelman E, Thomaes S, Nelemans SA, Orobio de Castro B, Overbeek G, Bushman BJ. Origins of narcissism in children. *Proc Natl Acad Sci U S A*. 2015;112(12):3659-3662. doi:10.1073/pnas.1420870112.

Cain, N. M., Pincus, A. L., & Ansell, E. B. (2008). Narcissism at the crossroads: Phenotypic description of pathological narcissism across clinical theory, social/personality psychology, and psychiatric diagnosis. *Clinical Psychology Review, 28* (4), 638–656.

Caligor, E., Levy, K. N., & Yeomans, F. E. (2015). Narcissistic personality disorder: Diagnostic and clinical challenges. American Journal of Psychiatry, 172(5), 415-422.

Carter, L. (Host). (2022, September 27). How to Detect Covert Narcissism. [Audio Podcast Episode]. *Surviving Narcissism with Dr. Les Carter.*

Davis, A. M., & Ernst, R. (2019). Racial gaslighting. Politics, Groups, and Identities, 7(4), 761-774.

Dhawan, N., Kunik, M. E., Oldham, J., & Coverdale, J. (2010). Prevalence and treatment of narcissistic personality disorder in the community: a systematic review. Comprehensive Psychiatry, 51(4), 333-339.

Drescher, Anna. "Narcissistic Baiting Examples & How To Respond." Simply Psychology, Simply Psychology, 23 Jan.2024,https://www.simplypsychology.org/narcissistic-baiting-and-how-to-respond.html.

Dr. Daniel Fox, Licensed Psychologist

Dr. Ramani, Clinical Psychologist

Durvasula, R. (2018, November 15). Gaslighting by Tribe. *Psychology Today*. Retrieved 2023, March 30, from: https://www.psychologytoday.com/gb/blog/guide-better-relationships/201811/gaslighting-tribe.

Foster, J. D., & Campbell, W. K. (2007). Are there such things as "'Narcissists'" in social psychology? A taxometric analysis of the Narcissistic Personality Inventory. *Science Direct*, 1321–1332.

Green, A., & Charles, K. (2019). Voicing the victims of narcissistic partners: A qualitative analysis of responses to narcissistic injury and self-esteem regulation. *Sage Open*, 9(2), 2158244019846693.

Gunderson, J. G., Ronningstam, E., & Bodkin, A. (1990). The diagnostic interview for narcissistic patients. *Archives of General Psychiatry*, 47 (7), 676–680.

Guy-Evans, Olivia. "Covert Narcissist Traits & How to Respond." Simply Psychology, Simply Psychology, 24

Nov. 2023, https://www.simplypsychology.org/covert-narcissism.html.

Holy Bible, New International Version®. (2011). Biblica, Inc.® (Original work published 1973, 1978, 1984). Used by permission. All rights reserved worldwide.

https://childrenofnarcissists.org.uk/the-narcissistic-family-system/

https://local21news.com/news/local/suspended-judge-sonya-mcknight-allegedly-shot-her-ex-boyfriend-in-the-face-a-timeline

https://medium.com/@empathicwarrior/how-do-narcissist-treat-their-stepchildren 059146987cc5#:~:text=Narcissists%20typically%20crave%20control%20and,their%20personal%20growth%20and%20autonomy.

https://www.my3bc.com/when-did-god-no-longer-allow-marriage-between-close-relatives/

https://www.neverthirsty.org/bible-qa/qa-archives/question/what-does-the-bible-say-about-marrying-your-first-cousin/

https://www.witf.org/2019/05/15/shooting-by-harrisburg-district-judge-turned-over-to-attorney-generals-office/

Jodi Clarke, MA, LPC/MHSP

Johnson, V. E., Nadal, K. L., Sissoko, D. G., & King, R. (2021). "It's not in your head": Gaslighting, 'splaining, victim blaming, and other harmful reactions to microaggressions. Perspectives on psychological science, 16(5), 1024-1036.

Kacel, E., Enis, N., & Pereira, D. (2017, August 2). *Narcissistic Personality Disorder in Clinical Health Psychology Practice: Case Studies of Comorbid Psychological Distress and Life-Limiting Illness: Behavioral Medicine: Vol 43, No 3.*

Kohut, H. (1966). Forms and transformations of narcissism. Journal of the American Psychoanalytic Association, 14(2), 243-272.

Konrath, S., Meier, B. P., & Bushman, B. J. (2014). Development and Validation of the Single Item Narcissism Scale (SINS). *PLoS ONE, 9* (8).

Maserejian, N. N., Link, C. L., Lutfey, K. L., Marceau, L. D., & McKinlay, J. B. (2009). Disparities in physicians" interpretations of heart disease symptoms by patient gender: results of a video vignette factorial experiment. Journal of Women's Health, 18(10), 1661-1667.

Riggs, D. W., & Bartholomaeus, C. (2018). Gaslighting in the context of clinical interactions with parents of transgender children. *Sexual and relationship therapy, 33*(4), 382-394.

Ronningstam, E. (2010). Narcissistic personality disorder: A current review. Current Psychiatry Reports, 12(1), 68-75.

Skodol, A. E., Bender, D. S., & Morey, L. C. (2014). Narcissistic personality disorder in DSM-5. Personality

Disorders: Theory, Research, and Treatment, 5 (4), 422.

Stark, C. A. (2019). Gaslighting, misogyny, and psychological oppression. The Monist, 102(2), 221-235.

Stinson, F. S., Dawson, D. A., Goldstein, R. B., Chou, S. P., Huang, B., Smith, S. M., ... & Grant, B. F. (2008). Prevalence, correlates, disability, and comorbidity of DSM-IV narcissistic personality disorder: results from the wave two national epidemiologic surveys on alcohol and related conditions. Journal of Clinical Psychiatry, 69(7), 1033-1045.

Substance Abuse and Mental Health Administration. (1999, May 17). *Psychodynamic Therapy*. Psych Central. https://psychcentral.com/lib/psychodynamic-therapy.

Sweet, P. L. (2019).The sociology of gaslighting. American Sociological Review, 84(5), 851-875.

Thomas, L. (2018). Gaslight and gaslighting. The Lancet. Psychiatry, 5(2), 117-118.

https://www.usatoday.com/story/news/nation/2024/02/18/suspended-judge-accused-of-shooting-her-ex-boyfriend/72651581007/

Wink, P. (1991). Two faces of narcissism. Journal of personality and social psychology, 61(4), 590.

Yakeley, J. (2018). Current understanding of narcissism and narcissistic personality disorder. BJPsych advances, 24(5), 305-315.

The Art of Mental Toughness

Employing Mental Strength in Martial Arts

By Raphael L. Vélez Lugo

Editor: Chanel Mullins
https://www.revisedink.com

The Art of Mental Toughness

By Raphael L. Vélez Lugo

Editor: Chanel Mullins https://www.revisedink.com

Formatted by: Monchaily Hendricks
https://www.xelbooks.com

First Edition, 2025
Printed in the United States of America

For information, please contact:
R. Vélez lakeridgetangsoodo@gmail.com

References

Ali, M. (n.d.). "He who is not courageous enough to take risks will accomplish nothing in life". *Source: Commonly attributed quote; often cited from his early speeches or general philosophical remarks.*

Aristotle. (n.d.). "We are what we repeatedly do. Excellence, then, is not an act, but a habit.". *Source: Commonly attributed quote; often cited from his early speeches or general philosophical remarks.*

Buddha. (n.d.). "The mind is everything. What you think, you become.". *Source: Commonly attributed quote; often cited from his early speeches or general philosophical remarks.*

Emerson, R. W. (n.d.). "Concentration is the secret of strength.". *Source: Commonly attributed quote; often cited from his early speeches or general philosophical remarks.*

Emerson, R. W. (n.d.). "Do the thing you fear, and the death of fear is certain.". *Source: Commonly attributed quote; often cited from his early speeches or general philosophical remarks.*

Ford, H. (n.d.). "Whether you think you can or think you can't, you're right.". *Source: Commonly attributed quote; often cited from his early speeches or general philosophical remarks.*

Frankl, V. (n.d.). "Between stimulus and response there is a space. In that space is our power to choose our response. In our response lies our growth and our freedom.". *Source: Commonly attributed quote; often cited from his early speeches or general philosophical remarks.*

Franklin, B. (n.d.). "Without continual growth and progress, such words as improvement, achievement, and success have no meaning." . *Source: Commonly attributed quote; often cited from his early speeches or general philosophical remarks.*

Gandhi, M. (n.d.). "Strength does not come from physical capacity. It comes from an indomitable will." . *Source: Commonly attributed quote; often cited from his early speeches or general philosophical remarks.*

King, B. J. (n.d.). "Champions keep playing until they get it right.". *Source: Commonly attributed quote; often cited from early speeches or general philosophical remarks.*

Lasorda, T. (n.d.). "The difference between the impossible and the possible lies in a person's determination.". *Source: Commonly attributed quote; often cited from his early speeches or general philosophical remarks.*

Mandela, N. (n.d.). "The greatest glory in living lies not in never falling, but in rising every time we fall.". *Source: Commonly attributed quote; often cited from early speeches or general philosophical remarks.*

Roosevelt, E. (n.d.). "You gain strength, courage, and confidence by every experience in which you really stop to look fear in the face.". *Source: Commonly attributed quote; often cited from her early speeches or general philosophical remarks.*

Tzu, L. (n.d.). "A journey of a thousand miles begins with a single step.". *Source: Commonly attributed quote; often cited from early speeches or general philosophical remarks.*

Unknown. (n.d.). "Real world mindsets don't fold under pressure. They adapt, they endure, and they finish what they start.".

Winfrey, O. (n.d.). "A mentor is someone who allows you to see the hope inside yourself.". *Source: Commonly attributed quote; often cited from her early speeches or general philosophical remarks.*

Wooden, J. (n.d.). "A good coach can change a game. A great coach can change a life." . *Source: Commonly attributed quote; often cited from his early speeches or general philosophical remarks.*

To my father, Miguel Rivera,

Your strength, wisdom, and unwavering support have shaped me into the person I am today. You instilled in me the values of discipline, perseverance, and resilience — qualities that have guided me through every challenge, both in life and in martial arts.

This book is a reflection of the lessons you've taught me, the sacrifices you've made, and the unwavering belief you've always had in me. I am forever grateful for your love and guidance and for always being my greatest source of inspiration.

This is for you Dad.

With all my love and gratitude,
Raphael~

ACKNOWLEDGMENTS

There are no words to fully express my gratitude to the people who supported me through this journey. Their guidance, dedication, and belief in me made *The Art of Mental Toughness: Employing Mental Strength in Martial Arts* possible.

Tracy Huff

Tracy, I cannot thank you enough for your invaluable support and guidance throughout this process. Your expertise, patience, and keen insights made writing this book a smoother and more enriching experience than I ever imagined.

Your encouragement and dedication helped shape this book into something truly meaningful. I am deeply grateful for your contributions, and it has been an absolute pleasure working with you. Thank you for your time, talent, and belief in this project — I could not have done it without you.

Chanel Mullins

Chanel, I am profoundly grateful for your exceptional editing work on this book. Your keen eye for detail, insightful feedback, and unwavering commitment to refining my words made all the difference in bringing this project to its fullest potential.

Your expertise and professionalism not only enhanced the clarity and flow of the book but also made the entire editing process a rewarding experience. I truly appreciate the time and effort you invested in helping me share this message with the world. Thank you for your hard work, patience, and dedication to excellence — I am incredibly fortunate to have had you as my editor.

Marla Vélez

Marla, I am deeply grateful for your unwavering support and care throughout my recovery journeys, including my most recent back surgery in December 2024. Your kindness and willingness to assist me during those times meant more than words can express.

Thank you for being there when I needed it most. I truly appreciate all that you have done.

Mom (Herda Rivera)

Mom, words cannot fully express my gratitude for everything you have done for me. Your love and support have been the foundation of my strength and success.

This journey — every achievement, every lesson I've learned — is a reflection of the values you instilled in me. Thank you for your sacrifices and for always believing in me.

With all my love and appreciation,
Raphael L. Vélez Rivera

FOREWORD

The Art of Mental Toughness: Employing Mental Strength in Martial Arts is more than a guide to martial arts training — it is a master class in resilience, discipline, and personal transformation. In this book, the principles of martial arts extend beyond the dojo, offering a blueprint for building mental toughness that can be applied in all areas of life.

In my years of experience, I've learned that mental toughness is often the dividing line between success and failure. Physical skill can take you far, but it is the mind that carries you through adversity, propels you past limits, and fuels your will to persevere. This book delves deep into the art of mental strength, combining time tested philosophies with modern strategies to help readers harness the power of their mindset.

What makes this book unique is its holistic approach. Through personal anecdotes, practical exercises, and insights from champions, *The Art of Mental Toughness* reveals the psychology behind success in martial arts and beyond. It explores the core tenets of focus, discipline, visualization, and resilience, offering tangible tools to help readers overcome obstacles and thrive under pressure.

The stories and lessons shared within these pages are a testament to the author's dedication to the martial arts community and their deep understanding of the human spirit. Whether you are an aspiring martial artist, a seasoned practitioner, or simply someone looking to cultivate strength in the face of life's challenges, this book will resonate deeply.

As you turn these pages, prepare to be inspired, motivated, and equipped with the mental tools you need to overcome adversity and reach your fullest potential. This book is a powerful reminder that the greatest battles are won not with the body but with the mind — a must have for every instructor and practitioner of martial arts.

— Pedro Vangas Jr.

President, Bi Sang Kwan Tang Soo Do Association MSCJ, US Army (retired), 10th Dan Tang Soo Do
9th Dan Korea Tae Kwon Do Moo Duk Kwan Association

February 2, 2025

Table of Contents

INTRODUCTION

In the echoes of my footsteps on the dojo floor and the quiet hum of focused breath, I found a path that shaped not only my body but the core of my being. This book is not just a collection of words on pages; it is a chronicle of my journey into the profound and transformative world of martial arts.

From the moment I tied my first belt around my waist, the dojo became more than a training ground — it was a sanctuary, where discipline turned into a way of life, and each technique whispered centuries old wisdom. Through the rhythm of strikes and the dance of sparring partners, I found a language beyond words. It communicated strength, respect, and self discovery.

As a martial artist, coach, and lifelong student, my life has been a tapestry woven with discipline, perseverance, and the relentless pursuit of mastery. In these pages, I invite you to join me on a pilgrimage through the landscapes of my martial arts discipline and beyond — a journey that traverses not only the physical realm but also the depths of the human spirit.

This book is more than techniques and forms. It's about triumphs, scars of defeat, lessons learned on and off the mat, and the evolution of a warrior spirit that transcends the dojo. Through my experiences, I hope to illuminate the universal truths embedded in the practice of martial arts — the profound lessons that extend beyond kicks and punches to touch the very essence of what it means to be human.

As we embark on this journey together, know that you're not just reading a manual on combat. You're stepping onto a path of self discovery, resilience, and the pursuit of becoming your best self.

Lying in that hospital bed, staring at the empty hallway, I reflected on the journey that led me here — a journey of decades, sacrifices, and countless highs and lows. I can't say that this journey has been enjoyable every day, but I can honestly say that it made me who I am today. I am grateful to be alive and well and to share my experience with you. This book is a collection of those reflections, woven together by my experiences and the lessons they taught me.

As Carl Jung once said, "Dreams are a way for the unconscious mind to communicate with the conscious mind."

In the same way, martial arts have been my bridge between the unconscious and the conscious. Through years of practice, the lessons ingrained in my body and mind surfaced during moments of reflection — like the one I had while lying in that hospital bed. It was there, in my most vulnerable state, that I realized the strength, resilience, and discipline I had built over the years were not just physical but deeply woven into the fabric of my being.

In a world of constant change and challenges, this book explores how martial arts can teach us the foundations of personal wellbeing, mental and physical conditioning, and the mysteries of adaptability in an unpredictable world. Join me on a journey to discover the keys to resilience in the world of martial arts.

"A journey of a thousand miles begins with a single step."
— Lao Tzu

Chapter 1: Pillars of a Champion's Mindset

Welcome to *The Art of Mental Toughness: Employing Mental Strength in Martial Arts*. This comprehensive guide will help you develop the mental resilience and strategic thinking essential for excelling in martial arts — and in life. This book uncovers the core components of a champion's mindset, offering practical techniques to help you reach your fullest potential.

In the summer of 2013, I prepared myself for what might be my final competition: the U.S. Capitol Classics China Open in National Harbor, Maryland. This prestigious event was one of the pinnacles of my martial arts career. I knew my time in power breaking, the sport I loved, was coming to an end, though I wasn't certain if this would be my final competition.

Not surprisingly to many, I won the Lightweight Power Breaking (Concrete) Division, taking first place and walking out with a beautiful trophy. This victory was bittersweet, marking my last competition with one of the greatest martial arts breaking teams in the world, Team Bergamo Schick Quattro. After that victory, I retired from professional martial arts competition, shifting my focus to learning, teaching, and sharing my knowledge with the next generation.

In 2014, I decided to attend graduate school to earn my master's degree in clinical mental health counseling. During this time, I was also working full time and going through a difficult divorce. The stress took a toll on my wellbeing, and my health declined. One morning in July 2014, I felt like I was having a panic attack. At the time, my partner took me to the emergency department, where I passed out. I woke up to the painful stab of an arterial line being inserted into my arm, followed by the nurse's muttered curse: "Fuck."

Having worked in a hospital for years, I knew exactly what she meant. As the nurse missed the injection, I remember thinking, *Just let me die.* The pain was unbearable. Then, the attending doctor leaned over and said words that shocked me to my core.

"Sir, you are having a heart attack."

I was in my early 50s. How could this be happening? I was shocked and angry with myself. As I lay there, many thoughts went through my mind — thoughts about my daughter, my family, friends, and the martial arts experience and knowledge I needed to share with my students and the world.

This book is a reflection of the knowledge, dedication, sacrifice, and triumph that martial arts — and life — have taught me. My journey is proof of the power of mental toughness, and through these pages, I hope to share that with you.

In martial arts, success relies on both physical prowess and mental fortitude. This book will take you on a journey of self discovery and improvement, highlighting the critical aspects of focus, discipline, dedication, resilience, perseverance, and adaptability. Master these pillars, and you'll not only strengthen your martial arts practice but build the mindset of a true champion — one capable of facing any challenge life throws your way.

Focus, Discipline, and Dedication

Imagine standing in the dojo, your mind laser focused, your body coiled with potential energy, ready to spring into action. In moments like these, focus, discipline, and dedication are not just concepts — they are the foundation of your training, the very tools that will push you beyond your limits. This book will teach you how to cultivate a routine that conditions both your mind and body, ensuring you stay committed to consistent practice. You'll learn how to adhere to structured routines that enhance your training, allowing you to excel in both practice and competition.

↦ *Personal Anecdote*
Building this level of focus and discipline took years of consistent effort. I first stepped onto the professional competition stage in the U.S. Open International Sport Karate Association (ISKA) World Martial Arts Championships in 1998. By 2003, I had honed my skills enough to take second place, but I knew I could push further. By 2004, when I first won the U.S. Open ISKA World Martial Arts Championships, my mindset was already set for me to win. I had trained extremely hard at the gym,

in martial arts class, and set up patio blocks on a weekly basis to break them. Furthermore, I worked on mindfulness exercises such as deep breathing exercises (diaphragmatic breathing) and meditation.

As I conditioned my body, my mindset was also being conditioned. I started to develop a focused mindset, which allowed me to enhance my performance. Martial arts training (forms, sparring, self defense, and weapons) helped me cultivate focus and concentration, and I quickly learned to master my techniques. Having strong focus, discipline, and dedication helped me achieve the ISKA Triple Crown Championship (U.S. Open ISKA World Martial Arts Championships, United States ISKA Championship, and North America ISKA Championship). In addition, I won the Arnold (Schwarzenegger) Sports Martial Arts Festival as well.

Raphael Vélez with all three 2004 International Sport Karate Association (ISKA) Triple Crown Championship belts: U.S. Open ISKA World Martial Arts Championships, United States ISKA Championship, and North America ISKA Championship.

In 2005, I returned to the Arnold Sports Martial Arts Festival to defend my 2004 title in the power breaking division. I decided to compete in the Creative Breaking Division, something I had stopped doing a couple of years back. During the beginning of my career, I competed in three to four divisions. I quickly learned I could either be looked at as a good breaker, or I could be the greatest lightweight power breaking competitor in the sport.

Therefore, I needed to change my mindset and focus on one event and train only for that event. Nevertheless, for the 2005 Arnold Sports Martial Arts Festival, I broke away from this mindset.

Consequently, during my creative routine, one of my teammates set up 10 scallop blocks, which were supposed to be a palm break. Trusting my teammate, I didn't doublecheck the setup of my 10 scallop blocks. Mid routine, I realized they were set too high. I improvised, striking them with both forearms. The blocks shattered — along with my ulna in both arms. In that instant, I went from a champion breaker to a man grappling with physical pain and emotional defeat. This was one of the lowest points in my martial arts career — a moment that left me defeated and questioning my ability to continue. But martial arts has also taught me that resilience is born in adversity.

Through mindfulness, I rebuilt my mental strength, learning to silence the self-doubt and focus on healing, both physically and emotionally. I redefined my path, not through force, but through acceptance, patience, and unwavering determination. Resilience is the art of working through emotional pain and suffering, emerging stronger on the other side. It's not just about enduring hardship — it's about using that hardship as fuel to grow, adapt, and rise again, stronger than before.

Resilience and Perseverance

Picture yourself facing a formidable opponent or recovering from a significant setback. How do you bounce back? Focus and discipline are essential, but what happens when things don't go as planned? How do you stay motivated when faced with setbacks? This is where resilience comes in, combined with perseverance. Together, they form the mental armor that allows you to push forward, no matter the obstacle, helping you maintain your focus on goals and keeping your motivation high. You'll read about inspiring stories, such as recovering from serious injuries and returning stronger, showcasing the power of a resilient mind.

Adaptability

In martial arts, the ability to adapt is crucial. I learned this firsthand in a sparring session where I faced an opponent with a completely different fighting style. My usual techniques failed, and I quickly realized that sticking rigidly to one approach would only lead to defeat. I had to adjust — both my mindset and my strategy. The same holds true in life. Being adaptable enables you to handle any challenge, whether it's a new opponent in the ring or an unexpected twist in your personal journey. This section will guide you through developing an adaptable mindset, preparing you to handle any curveball thrown your way. By learning to be flexible, you'll enhance your readiness and effectiveness in various scenarios.

Focus, discipline, and dedication lay the foundation for any martial artist, but resilience, perseverance, and adaptability are what separate the good from the great. These qualities allow you to not only overcome adversity but to evolve and excel, both in martial arts and in life.

"The greatest glory in living lies not in never falling,
but in rising every time we fall."
— Nelson Mandela

Techniques for Developing a Resilient Mind

Visualizing success is a powerful tool in building resilience. By mentally rehearsing successful performances, you create a mental blueprint that not only prepares you for victory but helps you bounce back from setbacks. Visualization trains your mind to see challenges as stepping stones toward success. Positive self-talk, another vital technique, helps replace negative thoughts with affirmations, boosting your confidence. We'll also explore goalsetting strategies, learning how to define clear, specific, and measurable objectives. By breaking larger goals into smaller, achievable milestones, you'll be able to track your progress and maintain motivation, building resilience through each step. These techniques are essential for developing a resilient mind, allowing you to focus on recovery, maintain motivation, and embrace challenges as opportunities for growth.

Focus and Clarity

Maintaining focus and clarity under pressure is a skill that can be developed. This book will guide you through practical exercises to improve concentration. For example, setting aside a specific time and quiet space each day for meditation or deep breathing can train your mind to stay focused under pressure. By incorporating mindfulness practices into your daily routine, you'll sharpen your ability to maintain focus and clarity even in high stress situations. You'll learn to visualize success and engage in focused activities that sharpen your concentration. Additionally, tips for high pressure moments, such as surrounding yourself with supportive people and simulating competition scenarios, will help you build familiarity and confidence.

Discipline and Routine

The path to mastery requires discipline and a well-structured routine. During my competitive years, I maintained a strict schedule of daily practice, balancing martial arts with mental conditioning. This consistency not only improved my techniques but built a mindset rooted in discipline. Through regular practice, you'll learn to push past plateaus and discover the transformative power of routine. Setting clear goals, creating a schedule, and practicing self-discipline are key elements discussed in this section. The impact of sleep, nutrition, and recovery on your performance and overall wellbeing will be explored, emphasizing their roles in maintaining discipline and preventing burnout.

Confidence and Self Belief

Building confidence is an ongoing process. This book will introduce methods to boost your confidence, such as using affirmations and keeping an achievement log. You'll discover how pre-competition routines and positive visualization can transform anxiety into confidence. By visualizing success and affirming your abilities, you'll learn to face fear head on and turn it into a source of strength, helping you step into the ring with assurance. The importance of self-belief in facing formidable opponents and managing fear and anxiety will also be covered, illustrating how confidence leads to better performance.

Emotional Regulation

Emotions can be powerful allies or formidable adversaries. This section will guide you on managing your emotions effectively. You'll discover how to create personal spaces for relaxation and mental recovery. Techniques like progressive muscle relaxation, where you tense and release each muscle group, will teach you how to control physical tension. Combined with deep breathing and positive Self-Talk, these practices will help you stay calm and composed in high pressure situations. Practicing gratitude will also be highlighted to focus on the positive aspects of life and enhance emotional regulation.

The Zone: Achieving Peak Performance

Reaching the zone, often called a flow state, is the ultimate goal for athletes. It's that magical moment when time seems to slow down, movements become effortless, and mind and body are completely aligned. In this book, you'll learn techniques to trigger this state, like mindful breathing, staying present, and using immediate feedback to adjust your performance. When you're in the zone, you perform at your best, free from distractions or doubt. This book will help you understand and achieve this state of optimal performance characterized by heightened focus and enjoyment. You'll explore mindfulness techniques to enhance present moment awareness, preparation routines to visualize success, and the use of immediate feedback to maintain focus and adjust performance. Achieving peak performance is about harmonizing your mind and body to perform at your best.

Conclusion

Throughout your journey in martial arts, you'll develop not just physical skills but the mental attributes that make a champion. Focus, discipline, resilience, and confidence are the cornerstones of this mindset, guiding you not only to success on the mat but to personal growth in every aspect of life. By training the mind to think optimistically and remain present, athletes can cultivate these key aspects and achieve excellence both on and off the mat.

Through practical exercises, personal anecdotes, and expert insights, the Pillars of a Champion's Mindset will equip you with the tools and strategies needed to harness the power of your mind and achieve your fullest potential in martial arts and beyond. Join me on this journey to develop a champion's mindset, where every challenge becomes an opportunity for growth and every goal becomes attainable.

"Whether you think you can or think you can't, you're right."

— *Henry Ford*

Chapter 2: Understanding and Developing Your Mindset

The Importance of Mindset in Martial Arts

In martial arts, as in life, mindset is everything. It shapes how we approach every challenge, how we recover from setbacks, and how we strive for success. Without the right mindset, even the most skilled martial artist can falter. Mindset encompasses attitudes, beliefs, and mental habits that shape how individuals perceive and approach challenges, setbacks, and goals. In martial arts, cultivating the right mindset can significantly influence performance, training, competition, and overall success and growth in life. A martial artist's mindset is built on five key pillars: discipline, focus, resilience, adaptability, and humility. These attributes not only shape how you train and compete but also guide your personal growth outside of practice. A strong martial arts mindset fosters continuous improvement, aids in overcoming challenges, promotes respect for others, and balances confidence and humility. Ultimately, mindset influences a martial artist's success, fulfillment, and growth inside and outside the dojo.

⊢→ *Personal Anecdote*
In February 2023, I faced one of the hardest decisions of my life. My mother's battle with dementia was worsening, and my father — once so strong — was diagnosed with idiopathic pulmonary fibrosis (IPF). The weight of their illnesses hung over me, and I knew I had to move to Florida to care for them, leaving behind my job, my home, and the martial arts school I had spent 13 years building.

During the COVID19 pandemic, my father, a Vietnam veteran, was diagnosed with IPF, a condition in which the lungs become scarred, and breathing becomes progressively difficult. He was given three to five years to live. This was another painful year for me. I retired from my job as a crisis intervention counselor, lost all my medical benefits, and sold my home and many personal belongings. Within four months of moving to Florida, my adult black belt student could no longer run the school, so I had to close my martial arts school.

I felt I had lost all my connections that took me 13 years to develop. Even in my 60s, this was one of the most difficult decisions I made. It was physically exhausting and mentally challenging.

Nonetheless, I am a strong believer in my God and who I am as a person. I learned that to have faith, you first need to have hope. I share this story to show how a strong mindset doesn't mean avoiding pain or hardship. It means facing it head on, believing in your ability to adapt, and maintaining faith in yourself, even when the path ahead feels uncertain. Even in the face of immense personal and professional loss, maintaining a positive, resilient, and hopeful mindset enabled me to navigate these challenges.

Challenges in Developing a Mindset

My journey as both a martial artist and a mental health counselor has revealed that the principles of mindset transcend fields. In martial arts, focus, discipline, and resilience are key to success. In counseling, those same principles — though expressed differently — are essential for personal wellbeing and effective client care. Developing a strong mindset in martial arts involves daily practice. Start by setting small, achievable goals that push you just beyond your comfort zone. Practice mindfulness before each training session to sharpen your focus, and reflect on your progress regularly to build confidence. Over time, this combination of reflection and discipline will shape your mindset and help you grow both in training and in life.

Specific Challenges and Strategies in Mental Health Professions

1. **Emotional Drain**
   Whether you're facing emotional challenges in the dojo or a counseling room, emotional resilience is essential. In both martial arts and mental health, practicing mindfulness and engaging in regular physical activity can help manage emotional stress, allowing you to stay focused and energized.

2. **High Levels of Stress**
   Psychiatric hospital settings can be high stress environments due to factors such as unpredictable patient behaviors and crises. Implementing stress management techniques, such as deep breathing exercises and regular breaks, is crucial.

3. **Vicarious Trauma**
   Mental health professionals may experience vicarious trauma or secondary trauma exposure, resulting in symptoms like PTSD. Regular supervision, peer support, and therapy can mitigate these effects. A famous psychiatrist once said to me: "Raff, everyone needs a therapist." If you feel like talking to someone, find a professional such as a counselor, social worker, or a mental health therapist. It is never too late to find help.

4. **Workload and Responsibilities**
   Heavy workloads, long hours, and demanding responsibilities contribute to mental drainage. Time management skills and setting realistic boundaries are essential to maintain balance.

5. **Boundary Issues**
   Maintaining professional boundaries all while still providing compassionate care can be challenging, but it is crucial. Clear communication and setting limits can help manage this balance.

6. **Lack of Self Care**
   Prioritizing patients' needs over personal wellbeing can lead to neglect of selfcare practices. Integrating self-care routines, such as exercise, hobbies, and reading positive books is vital for long-term wellbeing.

During my time as a mental health counselor, I was also a martial arts instructor. I thought my mindset was strong until I entered the mental health field and discovered its fragility. The mental health field helped me develop a strong mindset and understand people better, making me a better coach. You don't need to be a mental health counselor to develop a strong mindset; however, understanding mental health can enhance your coaching abilities.

Conclusion

A strong mindset is the foundation of success, both in martial arts and in life. It's built through discipline, focus, resilience, and a willingness to adapt. By embracing challenges and learning from setbacks, you'll not only improve your martial arts performance — you'll grow as a person, ready to face any challenge that comes your way. By understanding the importance of attributes like discipline, focus, resilience, adaptability, and humility, and by learning from personal experiences and challenges, we can cultivate a mindset that fosters continuous improvement and overall growth. Balancing technical knowledge with personal anecdotes provides a comprehensive understanding of the power of mindset, helping martial artists succeed in practice and the real world.

"Strength does not come from physical capacity. It comes from an indomitable will."

— Mahatma Gandhi

Chapter 3: Coaching a Champion Mindset

In martial arts, mindset isn't just important — it's everything. It's the driving force behind how athletes train, compete, and push through the toughest challenges. While physical skills are essential, it's often the mental game that separates champions from the rest. It encompasses the mental attitude, beliefs, and psychological traits that shape how an athlete trains, competes, and overcomes challenges. A strong mindset is often the difference between winning and losing, not just in competition but throughout the entire training journey.

As an instructor, your role goes far beyond physical training. The techniques you teach on the mat are only part of the equation — instilling the mental attributes that shape a champion is equally critical. It's the mental skills that help students push past their limits and grow into true martial artists. Below, we explore the key components of a champion's mindset and offer practical strategies for coaching these essential qualities.

Key Components of a Champion's Mindset

1. **Focus and Concentration**
   Teach your students the power of intense focus through exercises like silent sparring, where they concentrate fully on their movements and responses without verbal instruction. Encourage them to meditate or practice breathing techniques before class to hone their mental clarity. This type of training helps them react quickly and stay composed in fast paced competitions. At the peak of my career, my focus and concentration were unshakeable, and it made all the difference in my performance.

2. **Confidence and Self Belief**
   Confidence comes from experience and belief in one's abilities. Reinforce confidence by setting small, achievable goals for your students and celebrating each milestone. Encourage them to take calculated risks in controlled sparring sessions and remind them failure is just another step toward growth. When they see progress,

their self belief will naturally strengthen. Confident athletes push themselves further and perform at their best under pressure. When I broke 16 blocks on stage, it required 100% confidence — a testament to the importance of believing in oneself.

3. **Resilience and Perseverance**
Help your students develop mental toughness to withstand discomfort, setbacks, and failures. Mental resilience is built in the face of adversity. It allows athletes to bounce back from defeats and persevere through tough training. I've faced numerous setbacks in martial arts, college, marriage, and life, but resilience has always helped me rise again. Share stories like this with your students — show them setbacks are just stepping stones to success.

4. **Emotional Regulation**
Emotional control is key to staying calm under pressure. Teach your students techniques like progressive muscle relaxation or deep breathing to help them manage anxiety before competition. Role playing intense sparring scenarios where they're under pressure can also help them practice staying calm and composed, no matter the situation. Staying calm and composed is crucial for making effective decisions and reacting appropriately in high pressure environments.

5. **Adaptability and Problem Solving**
Martial arts competitions are dynamic and unpredictable. Adaptability is about being ready for anything. During sparring, have your students switch opponents frequently, requiring them to adjust their strategy in real time. You can also mix up their training routines, challenging them with unfamiliar drills. The ability to quickly adapt to changing conditions is what sets apart the best competitors. Adaptability was key to my success, especially when competing against larger, stronger opponents.

6. **Self Discipline and Motivation**
    Self discipline was something I had to cultivate over years of training, especially when I lacked outside support. When family or work pressures pulled me away from martial arts, it was my discipline that kept me on track. I encourage my students to create personal routines, to practice even when they're tired, and to set up a system of rewards for themselves. Building habits is the key to long-term success. Emphasize the importance of regular training and healthy habits. I struggled with motivation, especially when competing without family support, but surrounding myself with positive people and reading self help books helped me stay focused.

7. **Visualization and Mental Imagery**
    Guide your students through a simple visualization exercise. Have them close their eyes, breathe deeply, and imagine walking into the ring or stage. They should visualize every detail — the sounds, the lights, the feel of the mat beneath their feet. Then, have them picture themselves executing a flawless performance. Visualization primes the mind for success and helps build confidence before they even step onto the mat or stage. By vividly imagining themselves performing their best, athletes can enhance their skills and prepare mentally for competition. This skill was vital throughout my career and continues to benefit me today.

8. **Coachability**
    Coachability was a critical part of my journey. I remember being corrected repeatedly on a technique I thought I had mastered, and it wasn't easy to accept I needed to change. But being open to feedback allowed me to grow faster than I ever would have if I had resisted. Encourage your students to view feedback not as criticism but as an opportunity for growth. The most coachable students are often the ones who become champions. Being receptive to coaching is essential for continuous improvement. I always valued feedback, as it pushed me to refine my skills and strive for excellence.

    "The mind is everything. What you think, you become."
    — Buddha

Developing Resilience: Techniques and Strategies

Resilience is the mental toughness that allows athletes to push through challenges, setbacks, and failures. In martial arts, developing resilience is key to not only improving your techniques but also mastering the mental game that keeps you going when the going gets tough. Here are some techniques to help your students build a resilient mindset:

1. **Positive Self Talk**
    Help your students develop a habit of positive self talk by having them identify recurring negative thoughts and consciously replacing them with affirmations. For example, if they find themselves thinking, *I'm not strong enough*, they can counter it with *I've trained for this, and I'm ready*. Encourage them to create a personal list of affirmations and repeat them regularly, especially before challenging tasks.

2. **Setting Specific Goals**
    Guide your students to set specific, measurable goals. For example, instead of a vague goal, like to get better at sparring, help them set a goal with tangible results, like improving reaction time by 10% over the next three weeks. Break that goal down into smaller steps, such as focusing on speed drills twice a week or analyzing sparring footage. This process gives them clear milestones to track and celebrate along the way.

3. **Embracing Failure**
    Teach your students that failure is not a setback but a stepping stone to success. After a loss or a mistake, have them sit down and reflect on what went wrong — what could they have done differently? Use that reflection to adjust their training. Share your own experiences with failure and how it forced you to become better, reminding them that even the greatest champions face defeat before they achieve greatness.

4. **Seeking Support**

   Encourage your students to actively seek out a support network. Suggest they find training partners who challenge and motivate them, attend workshops or seminars to connect with like-minded athletes, and identify mentors who can offer guidance. Remind them resilience isn't built alone — it's strengthened through the support and feedback of those around you.

5. **Mindfulness Practices**

   Incorporate mindfulness into your students' training by beginning each session with a few minutes of focused breathing or meditation. Teach them to concentrate on their breath before a sparring match or competition, which helps calm their nerves and brings their mind to the present. This practice not only helps manage stress but also sharpens focus for peak performance.

Personal Anecdote: Competing As a Lightweight

Resilience isn't just a mental skill — it's something I had to embody throughout my martial arts career, especially when I faced physical disadvantages. Let me share a personal story that illustrates the importance of resilience in the face of overwhelming odds.

In the late 1990s, I stepped onto the stage of power breaking as a lightweight — a daunting challenge in a sport dominated by much larger and stronger athletes. My competitors often towered over my 5 foot, 4 inch (162.56 cm) frame and 168 pounds (76.2 kg), with many exceeding six feet in height and weighing over 200 pounds.

Every match was a test of my mental resilience, not just my physical strength. I had to believe in my ability to win, even when the odds seemed stacked against me. Each time I faced a larger opponent, I reminded myself that skill, strategy, and mental toughness could overcome size and power. This experience taught me that true strength comes from within — the ability to stay focused, adapt, and push forward, no matter the challenge.

Clinton Murphy and Raphael Vélez at the 2002 ISKA Connecticut State Championship.

When I first entered the world of martial arts, I didn't have the mindset necessary to believe in myself, let alone succeed. My doubts held me back, but I knew something had to change. By developing self-awareness and mental toughness, I began to understand that success starts in the mind. Visualization and positive self-talk became my lifelines, helping me build the confidence and resilience I needed. Visualization allowed me to mentally rehearse success before it happened. I would picture myself executing techniques perfectly, overcoming any doubts that crept in. Positive self-talk replaced the internal narrative of *I can't* with *I've got this.* Over time, these mental tools shifted my perception — my smaller stature was no longer a disadvantage but a chance to refine my technique, adapt my strategy, and ultimately succeed.

Challenges in Coaching Students with Behavioral Disorders

Just as I had to overcome my own mental hurdles, I've faced significant challenges as a coach working with students who struggle with behavioral disorders. Coaching students with oppositional defiant disorder (ODD) is a unique challenge, but it has also provided some of the most rewarding experiences of my career. These students often display patterns of defiance and anger that can disrupt a martial arts class. However, martial arts can offer significant benefits for managing these behaviors.

· Structured Environment

Martial arts offers the discipline and structure that students with ODD need. Establish clear, nonnegotiable rules from the very start of class, and ensure these rules are consistently enforced. Incorporate predictable routines — like starting each class with a bow and mindfulness exercise — to provide stability. Over time, this structure helps these students manage their emotions and behaviors more effectively.

· **Anger Management**

Techniques for managing emotions, such as deep breathing and mindfulness, are integral to martial arts and can aid ODD students in regulating their moods.

· **Conflict Resolution**

Teaching nonviolent conflict resolution strategies helps ODD students handle disputes constructively, promoting healthier relationships.

· **Positive Behavior Reinforcement**

Positive reinforcement can be a game changer for students with ODD. Recognize even small successes, like mastering a basic stance or showing restraint in a sparring match. Verbal praise, progress badges, or small rewards can go a long way in boosting their self-esteem and motivation. The key is to catch them succeeding, not just when they struggle.

A Personal Experience: Mario's Story

Years ago, I worked with a student named Mario who exhibited challenging behaviors typical of ODD. Initially, I hoped martial arts would help him channel his energy positively. However, as Mario grew older and his behavior became more disruptive, the situation escalated. One evening, Mario's defiance came to a boiling point. He challenged me to a fight in front of the class, and in that moment, I made a decision I later regretted. I agreed, thinking it would be a lesson in discipline and respect. But the outcome was far from what I expected. Instead of earning his respect, I realized too late his behavior was a cry for help — one I had missed. The encounter left me in deep reflection on the role of a coach in guiding, not just disciplining, troubled students.

Although I intended to teach him about discipline, the experience ended up being a profound lesson for me. Mario's behavior was a signal of deeper issues I failed to address, and my approach didn't acknowledge his underlying distress. That night taught me more than I could have imagined. The legal challenges that followed were a wakeup call, and I realized the importance of early intervention, clear boundaries, and seeking external support when necessary. If faced with the same situation today, I would have removed Mario from the class immediately and worked with his parents and mental health professionals to address the underlying issues before it escalated further.

When coaching students with complex emotional needs, early intervention is key. If a student exhibits ongoing disruptive behavior, address it privately with them early on. Set firm boundaries and communicate these to both the student and their parents. Don't hesitate to involve counselors or behavioral specialists if the behavior persists. The earlier you intervene, the greater the chance of guiding the student toward positive growth.

Conclusion

Coaching a champion mindset means going beyond physical techniques — it's about nurturing the mental and emotional strength athletes need to thrive in their daily lives and in practice. Whether it's teaching resilience to a competitive student or guiding a troubled one through their behavioral challenges, the role of a coach is to help shape the person behind the martial artist. Recognize the signs of distress early, set firm boundaries, and never hesitate to seek support when needed. Every challenge you face as a coach not only helps your students grow but helps you become a better leader and mentor.

Being an effective coach requires a deep understanding of the mental and emotional aspects of performance. By focusing on resilience, adaptability, and the psychological attributes that define success, you can help your students navigate challenges, stay motivated, and continuously improve — both in martial arts and in life.

Every experience, whether positive or challenging, contributes to your growth as a coach and to the development of your students. Knowledge, especially hard earned through experience, is a powerful tool in shaping a resilient and successful mindset.

"A good coach can change a game. A great coach can change a life."

— John Wooden

Chapter 4: Confidence and Self Discipline in Martial Arts

Confidence and self-discipline are the twin pillars of success in martial arts. They not only sharpen performance in the dojo but also transform how students approach challenges in everyday life. As an instructor, your role goes beyond teaching physical techniques — you have the power to shape your students' minds, helping them unlock their potential through these crucial traits, and you play a vital role in fostering these qualities. This chapter explores practical strategies to help you build confidence and cultivate self-discipline in your students, supported by personal anecdotes, psychological insights, and actionable tools.

The Interconnectedness of Confidence and Self Discipline

Confidence is the belief in one's abilities and the conviction that success is within reach. It is forged through consistent practice, mastery of techniques, and the power of positive self talk. Equally essential is self discipline, the bedrock of martial arts, which lays the foundation for continuous growth and unwavering improvement.

Confidence and self discipline are deeply intertwined. Confidence grows when students see the results of disciplined, consistent practice. At the same time, self discipline is strengthened when students believe in their ability to succeed. Together, they create a positive feedback loop — confidence fuels discipline, and discipline reinforces confidence — driving progress and elevating performance both in the dojo and in life.

As a martial arts instructor or coach, your role in cultivating these traits is both crucial and transformative. When I first started my martial arts journey, my confidence was shaky, and self discipline felt like an uphill battle. I remember staring at a concrete block, my mind filled with doubt — could I really break this? The fear of failure gripped me, and it took everything I had to push through. But with every small victory, my confidence grew, and I began to understand the power of persistence.

Each broken block became a testament to the strength that lay within, waiting to be unlocked. Yet, I have always believed that no one is truly self made; there is always someone or something that inspires us to surpass the limits we once thought insurmountable.

Building Confidence

1. Skill Mastery
Confidence is built through mastering small, achievable steps. As an instructor, break down complex techniques into smaller components for your students to master one at a time. For example, when teaching a complex form, focus first on stance, then transitions, and finally on the flow between movements. Celebrate each improvement, no matter how small. This step by step mastery builds confidence incrementally and gives students a clear sense of their progress. Provide a structured curriculum where students can see their progress through belt advancements or skill certifications. This visible progression is a powerful confidence booster.

↦ *Personal Anecdote*
I remember teaching my Little Tiger's class (ages three to six) their first form. Instead of starting them with a complex form that has 20 movements, I introduced them to a basic form with just eight movements, called KiBon, which means "the fundamental basic" in Korean. By focusing on mastering this fundamental form, the students gradually built their confidence. This same approach works with older students who struggle with basic techniques. By focusing on mastering one technique at a time and celebrating each small victory, they gradually build their confidence.

2. Positive Reinforcement
Create a supportive environment where effort and achievements are consistently recognized. In my classes, I've seen the impact of positive reinforcement firsthand. After a tough sparring match, even a simple "Well done" can uplift a student and motivate them to push harder next time. I also use small reward systems like achievement badges for younger students, recognizing their effort in mastering new techniques. By acknowledging their progress, we encourage them to keep striving for improvement. Share stories of students who transformed through encouragement.

↦ *Scientific Insight*
Positive reinforcement works by stimulating the brain's reward centers, releasing dopamine, which reinforces the behavior and encourages students to pursue their art. For positive reinforcement to be effective, it's essential to give feedback immediately after the desired behavior occurs. This helps students clearly associate their effort with the positive outcome, making them more likely to repeat the behavior.

↦ *Personal Experience*
During my time as a mental health counselor, I frequently used positive reinforcement to encourage my clients to stay committed to their treatment plans. The immediate praise or rewards following their efforts helped boost their motivation and progress, similar to how martial arts students thrive on positive feedback.

3. Public Performances and Competitions
Help your students prepare for public performances by guiding them through mental exercises. Teach them to visualize not just the physical execution of their techniques but also the feeling of confidence they'll experience on stage or in the ring. Have them practice in front of small groups to gradually build up their comfort level. The key is preparation — both mentally and physically — so that when they step into the spotlight, they feel ready to shine. These preparatory events offer students the chance to showcase their skills, confront performance anxiety, and build confidence. Guide them through the preparation process, helping them visualize success and mentally rehearse their routines.

↦ *Expanded Technique*
Consider organizing mock competitions within the dojo to simulate the experience in a controlled environment. This helps students gain confidence before facing real audiences or opponents. For example, I often held small tournaments within my school, where students could compete against each other in a supportive setting. These mock events not only prepared them for larger competitions but also helped them build camaraderie and mutual respect.

↦ *Scientific Insight*
Research shows that visualization activates the same neural pathways in the brain as actual performance, making it a powerful tool for reducing anxiety and improving confidence in high pressure situations.

Cultivating Self Discipline

1. Routine and Structure

Consistency not only builds discipline but also creates a sense of security. For students, especially younger ones, knowing what to expect each day in the dojo fosters confidence. Structure gives them a safe space where they can focus on improvement without distraction. By developing a consistent training schedule, you're helping them internalize the discipline they need to succeed both inside and outside of class. Emphasize the value of regular practice and commitment. A structured and predictable environment, especially for children with mental health disorders, helps them feel safe and secure.

↦ *Personal Anecdote*
In my classes, I've seen how a consistent training schedule helps students internalize discipline. One student, Alex, initially struggled with attendance, often missing classes or arriving late. We set a routine and outlined clear expectations, which significantly improved his commitment to practice. Over time, his attendance became more consistent, and his skills noticeably improved.

2. Goal Setting

Help your students set SMART goals (specific, measurable, achievable, relevant, and timebound). For example, a short-term goal might be to improve their side kick speed by 10% over the next two weeks, while a long-term goal could be to earn their next belt within six months. Consider using a visible goalsetting chart in the dojo where students can track their milestones, such as mastering a new kick or advancing to the next belt level, giving them a tangible sense of their progress and reinforcing their discipline as they work toward their goals. For more advanced students, create a detailed roadmap outlining their journey from one belt level to the next, with specific milestones and deadlines. Teach them how to set realistic, achievable goals and create a plan to reach them. This process instills a sense of purpose and discipline as students work toward their objectives.

↦ *Scientific Insight*
Setting goals provides students with a clear direction, increasing motivation and focus. Achieving goals releases dopamine, reinforcing self-discipline and commitment to continuous improvement.

3. Self-Reflection and Accountability
Encourage your students to reflect on their training at the end of each session by introducing a reflection journal. Have them write down one thing they did well and one area where they want to improve. They can also be prompted to write about other topics, such as their training experiences or what they've learned. Over time, this habit fosters self-awareness and accountability as they begin to take ownership of their own progress and personal growth. By periodically reviewing these reflections with them, you can provide tailored feedback and help them stay on course.

Confidence and self-discipline are more than just traits — they are the keys to unlocking potential, both in martial arts and in life. As an instructor, you have the power to shape these qualities in your students, helping them not only master techniques but also develop the mental resilience and determination needed for lifelong success. By building confidence and fostering self-discipline, you're giving your students the tools to face any challenge throughout their life.

"You gain strength, courage, and confidence by every experience in which you really stop to look fear in the face."
— Eleanor Roosevelt

Integrating Life Skills

Martial arts is about more than just physical techniques — it's about shaping the character and habits of your students for success in all aspects of life. By integrating life skills like time management, resilience, and mentorship into your teaching, you not only help your students excel in the dojo but also equip them with tools that will serve them in school, work, and personal relationships. These skills are foundational to creating well rounded, confident individuals.

1. Time Management

Teach students the importance of time management by encouraging them to create weekly schedules that balance martial arts, schoolwork, and other activities. One effective technique is the time blocking method, where students allocate specific blocks of time for each activity. For example, encourage them to designate 30 minutes for homework before each training session. This structure can help them stay on track and prevent feelings of overwhelm.

↦ *Personal Anecdote*
One of my students, Jason, struggled with balancing his schoolwork and martial arts practice, often feeling overwhelmed. Together, we implemented a time blocking schedule, where he allocated specific times for homework, martial arts, and rest. After a few weeks, Jason saw improvements not only in his martial arts performance but also in his school grades. This structure helped him regain control over his time and boosted his confidence in both areas.

2. Resilience and Perseverance

Share stories of overcoming challenges and setbacks, both from your own experience and those of your students. Highlight the importance of resilience and perseverance in martial arts and life, encouraging students to stay disciplined and motivated even in difficult times.

↦ *Personal Anecdote*
I'll never forget the moment when I was told my broken arms would take months to heal. The initial shock was followed by frustration and even fear — would I ever get back to where I was? But as the weeks went by, I learned something invaluable. Each small victory in recovery, from regaining mobility to performing my first kick again, taught me the true

meaning of perseverance. It wasn't about rushing the process; it was about staying committed, even when progress seemed slow. I often share this story with my students to remind them that setbacks are part of the journey, and it's how you rise after the fall that defines you. Setbacks are not the end but a part of the journey. Overcoming these obstacles is what truly builds character and strength.

3. Role Models and Mentorship

As a martial arts instructor, you have the unique opportunity to model self-discipline, confidence, and resilience every day. Start by showing consistency — arrive on time, follow through on promises, and demonstrate respect for others. Encourage open communication with your students, making yourself available for advice or support, whether related to martial arts or personal challenges. Share your own stories of struggle and growth, letting students see that even coaches face obstacles. By being open and approachable, you create an environment where students feel comfortable seeking guidance.

To be an effective mentor, provide opportunities for students to take on leadership roles in the dojo, such as assisting in classes or mentoring younger students. Encourage them to reflect on how martial arts values — like perseverance and respect — apply to their school or personal lives. Check in regularly with students about their progress, both in training and outside the dojo, offering encouragement and advice on how to overcome challenges. Mentorship is about being there for your students, not just as an instructor but as a guide who helps them navigate life's ups and downs.

↦ *Expanded Insight*
Research shows that students are more likely to adopt positive behaviors when they see these traits consistently modeled by authority figures. By maintaining integrity, showing resilience in the face of challenges, and demonstrating commitment to personal growth, you set a powerful example that your students will strive to follow.

Conclusion

By integrating these life skills into your martial arts teaching, you're doing more than just creating strong martial artists — you're shaping resilient, confident individuals who are prepared to face any challenge. Remember, your role is more than teaching techniques. You're mentoring students in skills that will serve them for a lifetime. The greatest legacy you can leave as a coach is not in the medals your students win but in the character, resilience, and discipline they carry with them long after they leave the dojo.

"A mentor is someone who allows you to see the hope inside yourself."
— Oprah Winfrey

Chapter 5: Fear Management in Martial Arts

Fear is a natural part of martial arts training, whether it's the fear of getting hit in sparring, performing in public, or facing a more skilled opponent. But fear doesn't have to hold students back. When managed effectively, fear can become a powerful tool that drives growth and improvement. This chapter explores strategies to help your students not just confront their fears but transform them into strengths that fuel their success.

Understanding Fear

1. Acknowledge the Emotion
Recognize that fear is a normal response to perceived threats, whether it's anxiety about sparring, tournaments, or learning new techniques. Understanding that everyone experiences fear can help normalize the emotion and reduce its power.

↦ *Personal Anecdote*
Early in my teaching career, I had a student named Emily who dreaded sparring. Every time it was on the schedule, she would tense up, sometimes even making excuses to miss class. I knew that ignoring her fear wouldn't make it go away, so we started by simply talking about it. I reassured her that her fear was normal and even the most experienced martial artists face it. By acknowledging her fear, we took the first step toward normalizing it and turning it into something she could manage.

2. Identify Triggers
Encourage students to actively identify the specific moments when fear arises. Have them keep a fear journal where they note the exact situations — whether it's before sparring, during competitions, or when faced with learning something new. By writing down what they felt and when, students gain a clearer picture of their triggers.

This self-awareness is crucial in developing a targeted strategy to confront those fears and take control of their responses.

Confronting Fear

1. Gradual Exposure
Gradual exposure is key to conquering fear. For students afraid of sparring, start with shadowboxing to practice movements without contact. Next, introduce partner drills with no contact, allowing students to get comfortable with the presence of an opponent. Then, move on to light contact sparring before advancing to full contact scenarios. By building confidence at each level, students learn to face their fears step by step, making them less overwhelming.

2. Visualization Techniques
Visualization is a powerful mental tool. Have your students close their eyes and imagine themselves entering the ring, feeling calm and confident. Encourage them to picture the exact movements they'll use and to see themselves handling each challenge with poise. I've seen students overcome significant fear by practicing mental rehearsals where they picture every detail, from their breathing to the sounds around them. This mental practice gives them the confidence to perform in reality as they imagined it. Mental rehearsal can reduce anxiety and build confidence. Encourage them to imagine every detail — from their movements to their emotions — with a positive outcome.

↦ *Scientific Insight*
Visualization works by creating neural pathways in the brain that mirror those activated during actual performance. This mental practice can enhance physical performance and reduce anxiety when facing a real situation.

3. Controlled Breathing
Breathing techniques are one of the most effective ways to manage the physiological symptoms of fear, such as shortness of breath, rapid heartbeat (tachycardia), and a sensation of butterflies in the stomach. Once your students master diaphragmatic breathing (outlined below), encourage them to use it in moments of heightened anxiety — before stepping into the ring, during a sparring match, performing forms, or while preparing for a difficult technique. Controlled breathing slows the heart rate and sends a message to the brain that it's okay to stay calm, even when facing something intimidating.

Step-by-Step Guide to Diaphragmatic Breathing

1. Have students sit or lie down in a comfortable position.
2. Instruct them to place one hand on their chest and the other on their abdomen.
3. Guide them to inhale deeply through the nose, ensuring the hand on the abdomen rises while the chest remains still.
4. Exhale slowly through the mouth like you are fogging a bathroom mirror, feeling the abdomen fall.
5. Repeat for several minutes, focusing on the breath and the calming effect it has on the body.

Managing Fear

1. Reinforcing Positive Self-Talk

Encourage your students to develop their own positive affirmations. Begin by identifying common negative thoughts, such as, "I can't do this," or "I'm going to fail." Then, help them craft affirmations that directly challenge these beliefs. For example, "I've prepared for this, and I'm ready," or "I am strong and capable." Encourage them to repeat these affirmations regularly, especially before high stakes situations like exams or competitions. With time, this practice reshapes their mindset, replacing fear with confidence and self-belief.

I once had a student, Mark, who doubted his ability to break boards during belt tests. We worked on changing his internal dialogue from *What if I fail?* to *I've trained for this, and I'm ready*. This shift in mindset made a noticeable difference in his performance, and he successfully broke the boards on his first try.

2. Setting Realistic Goals
Setting small, realistic goals helps students build confidence gradually, which is crucial for managing fear. For instance, if a student's fear is public performance, start by setting a goal for them to perform in front of just one friend, then two, and eventually the class. Each small achievement boosts their confidence, showing them that fear can be managed step by step. When students realize they can overcome small challenges, it empowers them to face bigger ones with less anxiety.

↦ *Visual Aid*
Use the goalsetting chart so students can track their progress. For example, if a student's goal is to perform well in a tournament, the chart might include steps like mastering specific techniques, building endurance, and participating in mock tournaments.

3. Peer Support and Mentorship
Foster a supportive environment where students can share their fears and encourage each other. Pairing less experienced students with mentors or more experienced peers can provide guidance, reassurance, and practical advice for managing fear.

↦ *Scientific Insight*
Social support is known to reduce stress and anxiety. When students feel they are not alone in their fears and have a support system, they are more likely to confront and overcome their anxieties.

Practical Techniques

1. Dress Rehearsal
Walking through a future event helps students practice fear management in a controlled environment. For example, set up mock sparring matches where students can face off in front of a small audience, replicating the pressure of a tournament.

↦ *Expanded Technique*
You can also simulate unexpected situations, like having them spar against an opponent they haven't trained with before or dealing with a "what if" moment, such as equipment failure. These scenarios teach students how to handle fear inducing situations with confidence before they encounter them in reality.

2. Mindfulness Practices
Integrate mindfulness exercises, such as meditation or body scan meditation, to help students stay present and reduce anxiety. Mindfulness can increase awareness of fear responses and improve their ability to manage them effectively.

Step-by-Step Guide to Body Scan Meditation

1. Have students sit comfortably and close their eyes.
2. Guide them to focus on their breathing, taking slow, deep breaths.
3. Starting from the top of the head, ask them to mentally scan down through their body, noticing any areas of tension or discomfort.
4. Encourage them to breathe into those areas, relaxing with each exhale.
5. Continue the scan down to the toes, promoting a sense of calm and relaxation.

3. Regular Reflection

Encourage students to reflect on their experiences and progress. Keeping a journal where they note their fears, how they confronted them, and the outcomes can help them see their growth and identify effective strategies for future challenges.

↦ *Empowering Students*
Ask students to share their reflections during class discussions. This not only reinforces their progress but also fosters a community of shared learning where students can learn from each other's experiences.

Role of the Instructor

1. Modeling Calmness
As an instructor, demonstrate calm and composed behavior in stressful situations. Your demeanor can set a powerful example for students, showing them how to manage fear effectively.

↦ *Personal Anecdote*
In my own experience, I've found that staying calm during unexpected situations, such as a student getting injured during class, helps set the tone for how others react. When students see their instructor handling stress with poise, they are more likely to emulate that behavior.

2. Open Communication
Maintain open lines of communication with your students. Encourage them to talk about their fears and provide a safe space for these discussions. Understanding their concerns allows you to tailor your teaching approach to address their specific needs.

↦ *Expanded Technique*
Hold regular one-on-one check-ins with students, where they can discuss their fears and progress. This personalized attention can make a significant difference in how supported they feel.

3. Consistent Encouragement

Consistently encourage and support your students, celebrating their efforts and progress. Positive reinforcement can build their confidence and reduce fear over time.

↦ *Scientific Insight*

Research shows that consistent positive reinforcement strengthens desired behaviors. By regularly acknowledging students' efforts to confront their fears, you reinforce their bravery and resilience.

Conclusion

Fear management isn't about becoming fearless — it's about transforming fear into a source of strength. When students learn to control and channel their fear, they gain not only confidence in their martial arts practice but also resilience in their everyday lives. As an instructor, your role is to guide them through this process, showing them that fear is not an enemy to be defeated but a powerful ally that can push them to new heights. By helping your students manage their fears, you empower them to grow stronger, braver, and more capable of handling whatever challenges come their way.

"Do the thing you fear, and the death of fear is certain."
— *Ralph Waldo Emerson*

Chapter 6: Emotional Regulation in Martial Arts

Raphael Vélez teaching his Little Tigers class about emotional regulation.

Emotional regulation is one of the most vital skills a martial artist can develop. Whether it's handling frustration after missing a technique or staying calm during a high stakes competition, the ability to manage emotions directly impacts performance, focus, and growth. In martial arts, emotional regulation doesn't just lead to better results in the dojo — it helps shape resilient, disciplined individuals who can navigate the challenges of life with poise. This chapter explores strategies to help students understand, develop, and enhance their emotional regulation skills, equipping them with valuable tools for both martial arts and the broader world.

As a retired mental health counselor, I needed to develop this skill not just for martial arts but for dealing with mental health clients and other high pressure situations I encountered during my practice and career. While there isn't a one size fits all answer to developing emotional regulation for everyone, I want to share some techniques which were effective for me throughout my career as a mental health counselor, martial artist, and in my regular life.

Understanding Emotional Regulation

1. **What Is Emotional Regulation?**
   Emotional regulation refers to the ability to manage and respond to emotional experiences in a healthy and productive manner. It involves recognizing, understanding, and controlling one's emotions, especially in stressful or challenging situations. This skill is not about suppressing emotions but rather managing them effectively so they do not hinder performance or decision making.

2. **Why Is Emotional Regulation Important in Martial Arts?**
   In martial arts, emotions like frustration, anger, and anxiety can cloud judgment, disrupt technique, and even lead to injury if not managed properly. Whether a student is sparring with an opponent or pushing through a difficult training session, learning to regulate emotions ensures they stay calm, make clear decisions, and perform at their best. Emotional regulation calls for us to understand and control our emotions, using them as fuel rather than allowing them to become obstacles.

   ↦ *Personal Anecdote*
   One of my students, David, struggled with intense anger whenever he faced a challenging opponent. His emotions often led to reckless decisions during sparring, which put him and others at risk. By working together on emotional regulation techniques, David learned to recognize when his anger was rising and how to channel it constructively. Over time, his sparring improved significantly, and he became a more composed and strategic fighter.

Developing Emotional Regulation Skills

1. Self-awareness
Teach students to become more aware of their emotions by incorporating regular check-ins during class. For instance, after a challenging drill, ask students to pause and reflect by asking, "How are you feeling right now? Are you frustrated, anxious, or calm?" Encourage them to notice physical responses, like tension in their muscles or changes in their breathing. These small moments of reflection build emotional self-awareness, which is the foundation of emotional regulation.

↦ *Scientific Insight*
Research shows that self-awareness is linked to the activation of the prefrontal cortex, the part of the brain responsible for decision making and emotional control. By increasing self-awareness, students strengthen their ability to regulate emotions.

2. Mindfulness Practices
Mindfulness isn't just about relaxation — it's about staying present in the face of challenges. Integrate mindfulness exercises into training sessions by encouraging your students to practice mindfulness during sparring or intense drills. For example, during a sparring session, guide them to focus on their breath and the rhythm of their movements. If frustration arises, they can recognize it and let it pass rather than reacting impulsively. Mindfulness helps students become more attuned to their emotional triggers, allowing them to manage their responses rather than being controlled by them. Practices such as meditation, deep breathing, and body scanning help students stay present and calm, making it easier to manage their emotions.

3. Breathing Techniques
Controlled breathing is an invaluable tool in martial arts, especially during high stress moments like sparring or belt tests. Before a sparring match, guide students to practice the 4-7-8 breathing technique (outlined below) to calm their nerves and center their focus. During training, if emotions like frustration or fear start to take over, a few deep, controlled breaths can reset their mindset, bringing clarity and control back to the forefront. This simple practice can make the difference between losing composure and performing with confidence.

Step-by-Step Guide to 4-7-8 Breathing

1. Inhale quietly through your nose for a count of four.
2. Hold the breath for a count of seven.
3. Exhale completely through your mouth for a count of eight.
4. Repeat this cycle three to four times to induce a state of calm.

↦ *Scientific Insight*
Controlled breathing activates the parasympathetic nervous system, which helps to lower heart rate and reduce the physiological symptoms of stress. This makes it easier for students to stay calm and focused during intense situations.

Enhancing Emotional Regulation

1. Positive Inner Dialogue
Encourage students to replace negative thoughts with positive affirmations. Positive Self-Talk can shift their mindset, reduce anxiety, and improve emotional control. Phrases like, "I can handle this" or, "I am in control" can be empowering, especially in high pressure situations.

↦ *Personal Anecdote*
Lily, one of my most talented students, would freeze the moment she stepped onto the competition mat. Self-doubt consumed her — she'd often say, "I'm not good enough to be here." We worked together to change this internal dialogue. I encouraged her to practice positive Self-Talk every day, starting with simple affirmations, like, "I am prepared, I am strong, I belong here." She wrote these affirmations down, repeated them before each class, and carried them into competition. Over time, I saw a remarkable shift in her demeanor — Lily no longer hesitated, and her confidence radiated in every performance.

2. Emotional Visualization

Visualization is a powerful mental tool that can be seamlessly integrated into martial arts training. Before a competition or belt test, have students close their eyes and visualize themselves meticulously performing their techniques — feeling their feet move, hearing the sounds around them, and controlling their emotions throughout. Encourage them to picture how they will handle challenging moments, such as facing a stronger opponent or recovering from a mistake. This mental rehearsal primes their brain to react calmly and confidently in the actual scenario, reducing anxiety and improving performance.

↦ *Scientific Insight*
Visualizing activates the same neural pathways in the brain as actual performance because the brain interprets vivid mental imagery similarly to real life actions.

This happens due to a few key neurological mechanisms, such as mirror neurons and motor cortex activation, which in turn strengthen synaptic connections, reducing performance anxiety and enhancing focus and reaction time. By engaging the brain's motor, cognitive, and emotional centers, visualization becomes a powerful tool for enhancing performance before even stepping onto the stage or mat.

3. Goal Setting

Help students set realistic, incremental goals. Achieving small goals builds confidence and emotional stability, reducing the likelihood of becoming overwhelmed by larger challenges. Break down complex tasks into manageable steps, allowing students to see progress and maintain emotional balance.

↦ *Visual Aid*
Use the handy goalsetting chart for students to track their progress as it relates to their emotions. For instance, if a student's goal is to improve their emotions toward or during sparring, the chart might include steps like improving footwork and mastering defensive techniques to help them maintain composure with confidence under pressure.

Practical Techniques for Emotional Regulation

1. Emotional Check Ins
Start and end training sessions with quick emotional check-ins. Encourage students to share how they feel and any emotional challenges they might be facing. This practice promotes emotional awareness and builds a supportive community.

↦ *Expanded Technique*
Consider using a simple "emotion wheel" where students can point to or select the emotion they feel at the start and end of each class. This visual tool can help students identify and articulate their emotions more accurately.

2. Simulated Stress Scenarios
Create controlled stress scenarios that mimic the high-pressure environments of tournaments or belt tests. For instance, set up a mock sparring match where students must perform under the watchful eyes of an audience or against an unfamiliar opponent. Another effective strategy is to introduce surprise challenges during drills — such as asking students to continue sparring with a sudden change in technique focus or facing an unexpected rule adjustment. These scenarios help students practice emotional regulation in real time, making them better equipped to stay calm and focused under pressure.

↦ *Personal Anecdote*
I once organized a mock tournament where students faced a series of unexpected challenges, such as lastminute rule changes and surprise opponents. This experience helped them practice staying calm under pressure, and many reported feeling more prepared and less anxious during subsequent competitions.

3. Cognitive Reframing
Cognitive reframing helps students turn setbacks into opportunities for growth. For example, if a student struggles with a particular technique, instead of thinking, *I'll never get this*, encourage them to reframe it: *This is hard now, but every time I practice, I get closer to mastering it.* You can also reframe competition losses, helping students see them not as failures but as feedback. By shifting their mindset, students learn to view challenges as part of the learning process, building resilience and emotional strength.

Step-by-Step Guide to Cognitive Reframing

1. Identify the negative thought (e.g., I failed at this technique, I'm not good enough).
2. Challenge the thought by asking if it's entirely true and considering other perspectives.
3. Replace it with a more positive or constructive thought (e.g., I didn't get it this time, but now I know what to work on for improvement).

Role of the Instructor

· Modeling Emotional Regulation

Demonstrate emotional regulation through your behavior. Show calmness, patience, and control, especially during high stress situations. Your example sets a powerful standard for students to emulate.

↦ *Personal Anecdote*
In my experience, staying composed during intense situations, such as handling a disruptive class or dealing with a student's frustration, shows students the importance of emotional control. When they see their instructor manage emotions effectively, they are more likely to adopt similar strategies.

· Providing Feedback

Offer constructive feedback that focuses on effort and improvement rather than just outcomes. Positive, specific feedback helps students manage emotions like frustration and disappointment. For instance, instead of saying, "You didn't do that correctly," try, "You made progress on this technique, and with a little more practice, you'll master it."

· Creating a Supportive Environment

Foster an environment where students feel safe to express their emotions and seek help. Open communication and a supportive community are essential for developing emotional regulation skills. Encourage students to share their experiences and learn from each other.

↦ *Expanded Technique*
Hold regular group discussions where students can talk about their emotional challenges and how they are working to overcome them. This not only helps individual students but also builds a sense of camaraderie and mutual support within the group.

Integrating Emotional Regulation into Training

1. Routine Practice

Make emotional regulation a regular part of training, not just an occasional focus. Consistent practice helps students develop these skills more effectively. Incorporate emotional regulation exercises into warmups, cooldowns, and even during drills.

2. Collaborative Exercises
Use partner or group exercises that require students to communicate and manage emotions together. Team activities can build empathy, understanding, and collective emotional regulation. For example, pair students up for exercises where they must navigate challenges together, discussing their emotional responses and strategies.

I use a combination of exercises at my mental health counseling job and applied or modified them to fit my martial arts classes. Here are some collaborative exercises specifically designed for martial arts classes, helping athletes build communication, emotional regulation, and teamwork skills:

- **Blindfolded Partner Drills**

  - **How it works:** One student is blindfolded while their partner gives verbal instructions to guide them through basic techniques (e.g., footwork, blocking, or a simple kata).

  - **Purpose:** Develops trust, communication, and focus, teaching students to stay calm under pressure.

- **Controlled Reaction Training**

  - **How it works:** Partners take turns attacking slowly while the defender must stay calm, control their emotions, and respond efficiently. After each round, they discuss how they felt and what they could improve.

  - **Purpose:** Enhances emotional regulation and adaptability during combat situations.

- **"Switch Roles" Sparring**

  - **How it works:** One student plays the role of an aggressive fighter, while the other must remain defensive and manage their emotions without panicking. Afterward, they switch roles and discuss their experiences.

  - **Purpose:** Helps students understand different fight strategies and control emotions under pressure.

- **Energy Matching**

  - **How it works:** Partners practice light sparring but must match each other's energy and intensity without escalating. If one increases force, the other must verbally or physically signal to maintain control.

  - **Purpose:** Builds self-awareness, discipline, and the ability to adjust to an opponent's rhythm.

- **Emotional Reset Drill**
  - **How it works:** After a tough sparring session, students must practice deep breathing together, discuss their emotions, and shake off any frustration before the next round.
  - **Purpose:** Teaches resilience, emotional recovery, and sportsmanship.

3. Encouraging Reflection

Encourage students to reflect on their emotional experiences in their journal. Reflecting on what triggered their emotions, how they responded, and what they learned can reinforce emotional regulation skills.

Empowering Students

Ask students to set aside time after each class to write down their reflections. Encourage them to review these reflections periodically to track their progress and identify patterns in their emotional responses.

Conclusion

Emotional regulation isn't just a skill — it's a lifelong tool that helps students navigate not only the challenges they face in martial arts but also those they encounter in everyday life. By teaching your students to manage their emotions, you're giving them the keys to unlock their full potential as they navigate life. Empowering students to take control of their emotional journey ensures they will face future challenges with confidence, composure, and resilience. In the end, emotional regulation isn't just about improving performance — it's about building stronger, more self aware individuals.

"Between stimulus and response there is a space. In that space is our power to choose our response. In our response lies our growth and our freedom."

— Viktor Frankl

Chapter 7: Enhancing Focus and Clarity in Martial Arts

In martial arts, focus and clarity are the keys to mastering techniques and achieving personal growth. Without them, even the most talented students can struggle to reach their full potential. Whether it's sparring, learning a new kata, or staying composed under pressure, focus and clarity help students perform at their best. In this chapter, we'll explore how to cultivate focus and clarity in all students, including those with attention related challenges like attention deficit/hyperactivity disorder (ADHD), so they can thrive both inside and outside the dojo.

The Importance of Focus and Clarity

Focus and clarity are the cornerstones of effective martial arts practice. When students are focused, they can fully engage with the task at hand, whether it's mastering a new technique, sparring with a partner, or meditating in stillness. Clarity of mind allows them to make quick decisions, adapt to changing situations, and remain calm under pressure. These skills are crucial not only for success in martial arts but also for navigating the complexities of everyday life.

↦ *Personal Anecdote*
I remember working with a student named Jake, who struggled to stay focused during training. His frustration was palpable — every missed step felt like a setback, and it was affecting his confidence. By breaking down techniques into smaller steps and introducing mindfulness exercises, we worked on calming his mind. Slowly, his focus improved, and with it, his confidence. The transformation wasn't just in his technique — it was in how he approached challenges. He no longer saw mistakes as failures but as opportunities to refocus and grow.

Mindfulness and Meditation Practices

1. **Breathing Techniques**
   Teach students breathing exercises they can use right before sparring or while learning a challenging technique. Consider incorporating a "breathing break" during classes, especially before high intensity drills. For instance, before a sparring session, guide them through a series of deep breathing or diaphragmatic breathing to calm their minds and center their focus. This practice not only helps reduce anxiety but also sharpens their concentration, allowing them to respond more effectively in the ring or during drills. These techniques are especially useful when students feel overwhelmed or distracted.

   ↦ *Scientific Insight*
   Controlled breathing activates the parasympathetic nervous system, which helps reduce stress and increase focus. This physiological response prepares students to engage fully in their training.

2. **Meditation Sessions**
   Integrate short meditation sessions at the beginning and end of each class. These sessions can help students clear their minds, improve concentration, and prepare for focused practice by releasing any stress or distractions they brought with them. A simple, guided meditation focused on breathing or visualizing a calm place can be effective.

   During these sessions, students learn to let go of the mental clutter that can build up during the day, creating space for calm and clarity. After practicing this regularly, students often report feeling more present and grounded — not just in their training but when they leave the dojo as well.

   ↦ *Auditory Aid*
   Use a mindfulness timer app that gently signals the start and end of meditation sessions. This auditory cue helps students know when to begin and end their practice, keeping the session structured and focused.

You might start each class with a three minute guided meditation, asking students to focus on their breath and let go of distractions. End the session with a similar exercise, helping them transition smoothly out of the training mindset.

3. **Mindful Movement**
   Encourage students to practice each technique with full awareness, focusing on the precision of their stance, the positioning of their hands, and the flow of their breath. For example, while performing a kata or form, have them slow down each movement, noticing how their body feels as they shift from one stance to the next. This mindful approach not only sharpens their focus but also deepens their connection to the technique, allowing them to perform with greater clarity and control.

   ↦ *Personal Anecdote*
   In one of my classes, I introduced mindful movement by asking students to perform a simple kata with their eyes closed, focusing entirely on their breath and the sensation of each movement. Many students reported that this exercise not only improved their concentration but also deepened their understanding of the kata's flow and purpose.

   ↦ *Example*
   Incorporate mindful movement drills where students slow down their techniques, paying attention to each movement's mechanics. Encourage them to notice how their body feels during each phase of the movement, fostering greater awareness and control.

Structured and Focused Training

1. **Clear Objectives**
   Set clear and specific objectives at the start of each class and involve students in this process. For example, ask them what they aim to improve that day — whether it's mastering a particular technique or enhancing their balance. By actively engaging students in goal setting, you create a sense of ownership and accountability, which helps them stay focused and invested in the session's objectives.

At the start of a class, you might say, "Today, our goal is to perfect the roundhouse kick. We'll focus on the correct foot positioning, balance, and power." This clear objective helps students channel their attention toward specific aspects of their training.

2. Incremental Learning

Break down complex techniques into smaller, manageable steps. This methodical approach can help students concentrate on each component, building clarity and precision in their practice. For example, instead of teaching a complete kata in one session, break it down into sections, allowing students to master each part before moving on.

↦ *Scientific Insight*

The brain learns more effectively when information is presented in smaller chunks. This approach, known as "chunking," helps students process and retain information more efficiently, leading to clearer understanding and better performance.

↦ *Example*

When teaching a new kata, you might break it down into three parts: the opening stances, the middle sequence, and the closing movements. Spend time on each part before linking them together, ensuring that students understand and can execute each section with clarity.

3. Eliminating Distractions

Create an environment that minimizes distractions, tailored to different age groups. For younger students, this might mean a dedicated area for shoes and phones, while older students could benefit from a no phone policy in the dojo. Encourage everyone to practice leaving behind distractions, both physical and mental, before stepping onto the mat. This helps create a focused atmosphere where students of all ages can fully engage in their training.

⟼ Visual Aid
Post a "Focus Zone" sign outside the dojo as a reminder that the training space is a place for concentrated effort and mindfulness. This visual cue can reinforce the importance of maintaining focus during class.

⟼ Example
You can establish a no phone policy in the dojo, with designated areas for students to leave their devices (preferably on silent mode). This helps create a distraction free environment where students can fully immerse themselves in their training.

Mental Discipline and Visualization

· Concentration Drills

Incorporate concentration drills that challenge both mental and physical focus. For example, have students balance on one leg while holding a stance for progressively longer periods, focusing on their breath and posture. Start with 30 seconds and gradually increase the time as they build focus. To make it more challenging, introduce distractions, such as verbal commands or moving objects, to test their ability to stay focused. This helps students train their minds to remain steady even in chaotic environments.

⟼ Personal Anecdote
I once introduced a drill where students had to balance on one leg while holding a bokken (wooden sword) in front of them for several minutes. The goal was to remain completely still and focused. Initially, many students wobbled and lost balance, but with practice, they developed greater concentration and control.

⟼ Example
You might implement a "balance challenge" where students hold a stance for progressively longer periods, focusing on their breath and posture. This drill not only improves physical balance but also enhances mental focus.

You might also introduce a half circle balance trainer, placing the flat side on the floor with the dome side up (like a BOSU ball) or you can use another sturdy, half-sphere object.

A. Basic

Stance

Objective:
Stand on top of the half circle with both feet, knees slightly bent, and arms at your sides.

Instructions:

1. Step onto the half circle, positioning your feet shoulder width apart.
2. Engage your core muscles and maintain an upright posture.
3. Focus on keeping your balance for **30 seconds to one minute** without stepping off.
4. Once comfortable, close your eyes to increase the difficulty and challenge your proprioception.

B. Single Leg

Balance

Objective:
Stand on one leg while maintaining balance on the half circle.

Instructions:

1. Lift one foot off the half circle, bending your knee slightly on the standing leg.
2. Keep your hips level and avoid leaning too far in any direction.
3. Hold this position for 2030 seconds on each leg.
4. As you improve, extend the time or try dynamic movements like small leg lifts or arm raises.

C. Dynamic Movements (Squats/Lunges) — for advanced students

Objective:
Perform squats, lunges, or single kicks (front, side, back kicks) while balancing on the half circle.

Instructions:

1. For squats, stand with both feet on the half circle, engage your core, and slowly lower your body into a squat.
2. For lunges, place one foot on the half circle while the other foot stays on the ground. Lower into a lunge and return to the starting position.
3. For single kicks (e.g. front kick): Stand with both feet on the half circle. Keep your elbows tight and into your body. Lift one leg slowly as high as you can and slowly extend to front kick.
4. Focus on breathing and maintaining control and form while keeping balance.
5. Start with eight10 repetitions and gradually increase as you get more comfortable.

· Visualization Techniques

Teach students to visualize themselves not only executing techniques perfectly but also staying calm and composed during difficult situations. Have them imagine a high-pressure moment — like facing a stronger opponent — and see themselves handling it with clarity and confidence. Visualization strengthens both mental and emotional resilience, allowing students to rehearse not just the physical aspects of martial arts but the mental fortitude required to excel under pressure.

↦ *Scientific Insight*
Visualization activates the brain's motor cortex, the same area used during physical movement. Mental practice strengthens neural pathways, improving both focus and physical execution.

⟼ Example
Before a sparring session, guide students through a visualization exercise where they mentally rehearse a specific sequence of moves. Encourage them to visualize every detail, from their footwork to their breathing, helping to solidify the technique in their minds.

· Self-Reflection and Journaling

Encourage students to keep a training journal where they reflect on their progress, note areas for improvement, and set specific focus goals. This practice can help enhance clarity and provide a structured approach to their training.

⟼ Empowering Students
Ask students to review their journal entries regularly, looking for patterns in their focus and performance. This reflection helps them take ownership of their development and identify areas where they can improve their mental discipline.

⟼ Example
Provide students with a simple journal template that prompts them to reflect on each class. Questions might include:

- *"What was my main focus today?"*
- *"What distracted me?"*
- *"How can I improve my focus next time?"*

Addressing Specific Challenges for Students with ADHD (Attention Deficit/Hyperactivity Disorder)

1. Understanding ADHD

ADHD is characterized by a persistent pattern of inattention, hyperactivity, and impulsivity that interferes with functioning or development. Students with ADHD may struggle with sustaining attention, following instructions, and controlling impulses, which can pose unique challenges in a martial arts setting.

2. Martial Arts as a Tool for Managing ADHD

Martial arts can provide significant benefits for students with ADHD, including improved focus and concentration, enhanced self-discipline, and better emotional regulation. The structured environment and clear rules of martial arts training offer these students the consistency and support they need to succeed.

↪ *Scientific Insight*
Research has shown that physical activities like martial arts can help reduce ADHD symptoms by increasing levels of dopamine and norepinephrine in the brain, which are crucial for attention span and self-regulation.

3. Practical Strategies for Instructors

- **Shorter Sessions and Frequent Breaks:** Adapt training sessions to accommodate shorter attention spans.
- **Clear and Direct Instructions:** Use simple language with visual demonstrations to ensure understanding.
- **Positive Reinforcement:** Frequently praise efforts and progress to boost confidence and encourage focus.
- **Variety and Engagement:** Keep sessions engaging with varied activities that prevent boredom.
- **Individualized Attention:** Offer personalized support and guidance to help students manage their specific challenges.

↦ Personal Anecdote
I worked with a young student named Max, who had been diagnosed with ADHD. Max found it difficult to sit still and often lost focus during drills. By incorporating shorter, varied activities and providing consistent positive feedback, Max began to improve his concentration and control. Over time, he became more engaged in class and proud of his progress.

↦ Example
To keep Max engaged, I introduced quick, high energy drills followed by short breaks. For instance, we would do a fast paced kicking drill for two minutes, then take a 30second break before moving on to the next activity. This approach helped maintain his interest and allowed him to reset his focus between exercises.

Integrating Focus and Clarity into Training

1. **Routine Practice**
   Make focus and clarity a regular part of training, not just an occasional focus. Consistent practice helps students develop these skills more effectively. Incorporate concentration exercises into each session, gradually increasing the difficulty as students improve.

   ↦ Example
   Start each class with a focus warmup, where students spend five minutes on a concentration drill, such as balancing on one leg or performing a simple kata with their eyes closed. Over time, you can increase the complexity of these exercises to challenge their growing focus and mental discipline.

2. **Collaborative Exercises**
   Use partner or group exercises that require students to communicate and manage focus together. Team activities can build empathy, understanding, and collective focus. For example, a drill where one student practices while the partner provides feedback can enhance both participants' attention to detail.

↦ *Example*
Pair up students for a drill where one person performs a technique while the other observes and provides feedback on their focus and form. This not only encourages active engagement but also helps students learn to focus both as performers and as observers.

3. **Encourage Reflection**
   Encourage students to reflect on their focus and clarity in each class. What helped them stay focused? What distractions did they encounter? Reflecting on these questions in a journal or group discussion can reinforce the importance of mental clarity in martial arts.

   ↦ *Empowering Students*
   Guide students to set personal goals for improving focus, such as maintaining concentration during a specific drill or reducing distractions in class. These goals should be revisited regularly to track progress and celebrate successes.

   ↦ *Example*
   At the end of each class, hold a brief reflection session where students can share their experiences. Ask questions like, "What was the most challenging part of staying focused today?" Or, "What techniques helped you keep your mind clear?" This group discussion not only fosters a sense of community but also allows students to learn from each other's strategies.

Overcoming Common Challenges

· Handling Distractions

Even with the best strategies in place, distractions are inevitable. Whether it's external noise or internal thoughts, helping students learn to refocus after being distracted is key to maintaining clarity.

↦ *Example*
Introduce a "reset" technique where students take a deep breath and refocus their attention whenever they notice their mind wandering. Practice this technique regularly so it becomes a natural response to distractions.

· Addressing Frustration

Students, especially those with ADHD, may become easily frustrated when they struggle to maintain focus. It's important to acknowledge these feelings and provide strategies to manage them.

↦ *Example*
When a student becomes frustrated, encourage them to take a short break and use a breathing technique or visualization to calm down. Reassure them it's okay to have off days and that focus, like any skill, takes time to develop.

· Long-term Strategies for Sustaining Focus

Building focus and clarity is a long-term process. It's important to help students understand that while progress may be gradual, consistency will lead to significant improvements over time.

↦ *Example*
Encourage students to set long-term goals for their focus and clarity, such as being able to maintain concentration during an entire class without getting distracted. Periodically check in on these goals, adjusting them as needed and celebrating milestones along the way.

Conclusion

Focus and clarity are foundational to both martial arts and life. By consistently applying these strategies — whether through mindfulness, structured practice, or tailored support for students with ADHD — you can help your students build the mental discipline they need to succeed on the mat and beyond. The lessons they learn about concentration, patience, and resilience will shape their growth not only as martial artists but as individuals capable of facing any challenge with a clear mind and unwavering focus. Remember, focus is not just a skill; it's a mindset, and with it, anything is possible.

As instructors, it's important to remember the journey toward mastering focus and clarity is ongoing, but by offering personalized support and fostering a positive, focused environment, you can help your students build the mental discipline they need to excel.

"Concentration is the secret of strength."
— Ralph Waldo Emerson

Chapter 8: Discipline and Building Routines

Discipline has been the anchor of my journey. It's what keeps me on track, ensuring that each day, I move closer to my goals, no matter how small the steps might seem. Yet, the road hasn't always been smooth. Discipline demands consistency, and consistency often requires sacrifices — missed family dinners, fewer outings with friends, countless hours of solitary practice, and, sometimes, pushing through exhaustion when every fiber of your body wants to quit. Yet, through every sacrifice, the rewards — personal growth, mastery, and a deep sense of fulfillment — have proven worth it a thousand times over.

In martial arts, as in life, discipline and routines aren't just tasks to check off a list; they're the bedrock of mastery. Imagine a swordsmith, laboring day after day to perfect the edge of a blade. Each stroke is deliberate, each effort building on the last, until the blade is sharp enough to cut through steel. Discipline works much the same way. It's the force that drives you to practice even when you'd rather rest and the quiet resolve that keeps you going when the progress seems slow.

Building a new routine is like laying the groundwork for future success — it's a tool that transforms your daily habits into stepping stones toward your biggest goals. Whether you're training for a competition or simply striving for personal growth, a well designed routine becomes your roadmap to achievement.

In this chapter, we'll explore the essence of discipline, the art of crafting routines, and how to track, refine, and celebrate your progress along the way. My hope is that by the end, you'll not only understand the importance of discipline and routines but feel equipped to build them into your own life — no matter what challenges you might face.

The Essence of Discipline

What Is Discipline?

Discipline is the commitment to keep moving forward, even when the journey is tough, distractions are everywhere, and results seem distant. It's the quiet, steady force that keeps you on track, much like a river slowly carving its way through stone. In martial arts, discipline isn't just a skill you practice; it's a way of life.

Let me take you back to a cold winter morning years ago. I was tempted to skip practice — my bed was warm, and the idea of facing the frosty morning air wasn't appealing. But discipline isn't about what feels good in the moment; it's about what moves you closer to your goals. So, I got up, got dressed, and headed to the dojo. That decision, repeated countless times, is what has honed my skills, built my resilience, and ultimately defined my path.

The Role of Discipline in Martial Arts

In the world of martial arts, discipline is your most faithful companion. It pushes you to rise before dawn for early morning training, it strengthens your resolve during grueling drills, and it carries you through those moments when progress feels elusive.

Each punch, each kick, is a testament to your commitment — a promise to yourself that you won't quit, no matter how hard the journey gets. It's not just about skill; it's about the quiet power of showing up, day after day, even when it's hard.

1. **Consistent Progress**
   Like sharpening a sword with daily care, discipline ensures your skills are honed over time. Without it, progress would be inconsistent at best, and stagnant at worst.

2. **Enhanced Focus**
   Discipline acts as your internal compass, guiding you back to your goals whenever distractions threaten to lead you astray.

3. **Increased Resilience**
   Through discipline, you build mental toughness — the kind that helps you rise each time you fall, ready to push forward again.

Identifying Key Areas

Before you can build an effective routine, you need to know where to focus your efforts. Take a moment to reflect on your life and practice. Where do you most want to improve? Whether it's increasing flexibility, mastering a complex form, or finding more balance between work and training, identifying these key areas gives your routines purpose and direction.

Setting Clear Goals

Every journey needs a destination, and your goals serve as the compass that guides your efforts. But these goals are more than just targets — they represent your personal aspirations: your reasons for getting up every day and working toward something greater. By setting clear, specific goals, you create a routine that resonates with your deepest motivations, keeping you focused and inspired even on the toughest days.

↦ *Example*
Imagine you're a martial artist who struggles with balance during kicks. A clear goal might be to improve balance during sidekicks within three months by incorporating daily balance drills and core exercises.

Prioritizing Goals

Not all goals are created equal, and some require more immediate attention than others. Take the time to prioritize your goals, focusing on the ones that will have the most significant impact on your progress. Balancing short-term objectives with long-term aspirations ensures your routine addresses both immediate needs and future growth.

↦ *Example*
If you have a competition coming up, prioritizing techniques that need refinement might take precedence over building general fitness.

Understanding Your Current Habits

Before you can build something new, it's important to take a step back and reflect on what's already in place. What habits are serving you, and which ones are standing in your way? This reflection isn't just about efficiency — it's about understanding how your habits align with your goals and values. By developing this self-awareness, you can design a routine that not only builds on your strengths but also addresses the areas where you've struggled in the past.

↦ *Example*
If you realize that you often skip warmups, this is an area to focus on when creating your new routine. Understanding this habit can help you design a more comprehensive and effective approach.

Crafting Powerful Routines

· Designing Your Routine

Creating a routine is like crafting a custom suit — it needs to fit you perfectly. For example, if your goal is to increase flexibility, you might start with 10 minutes of stretching each morning and gradually add yoga sessions as you progress. If your aim is to improve endurance, a routine that begins with three days of interval training, followed by two days of strength work, provides balance. Remember, routines need to be both challenging and realistic, pushing you toward growth while still fitting into your life.

- **Specificity and Relevance**
  Tailor your routine to meet your exact goals. If endurance is your aim, include stamina building exercises like long-distance running or interval training. Your time is one of your most valuable resources, and how you choose to spend it determines your progress. Allocating specific times for each activity in your routine sends a powerful message to yourself — it's a commitment to your growth. Treat these slots as nonnegotiable appointments, moments that are sacred in your schedule. By dedicating time consistently, you're not only building a routine but also reinforcing the discipline that will carry you through challenges.

⟼ Example

If your goal is to improve flexibility, your routine should include targeted stretching exercises like dynamic stretches before practice and static stretches afterward.

Jessie working on his dynamic stretch before class

- **Structure and Consistency**
  Sustainability is key. It's better to engage in a 15minute focused practice every day than to commit to an intense regimen that you can't maintain. Remember, consistency always trumps intensity. The backbone of any successful routine is consistency. Create a structured plan that fits seamlessly into your daily life, making it easier to stick with over the long-term. The more your routine feels like a natural part of your day, the more likely you are to maintain it.

  ⟼ Example

  If you find mornings to be your most productive time, schedule your training sessions early in the day. This consistency will help form a habit that's hard to break.

- **Integration and Time Allocation**
  To turn your routine into a habit, integrate it seamlessly into your daily life. If mornings work best, make it a nonnegotiable part of your day, just like brushing your teeth. Effective routines require dedicated time. Allocate specific times for each activity in your routine, and treat these slots as nonnegotiable appointments with yourself. This reduces the risk of procrastination and helps establish a sense of rhythm and regularity.

  ↦ *Example*
  If you're working on your endurance, dedicate 30 minutes to running every Tuesday and Thursday at 7 a.m. This scheduled time becomes a regular part of your week, helping you stay on track.

· Starting Small, Building Strong

All great routines start small. Begin by identifying one area you want to improve — like flexibility or stamina — and commit to just 10 minutes a day. If flexibility is your focus, start with a basic stretching routine. As you become more consistent, gradually increase your time and add more advanced movements. The key is consistency, not intensity. Start small, let the habit settle in, and then slowly expand your routine as your progress builds momentum.

Big goals can be daunting, but breaking them down into smaller, manageable steps can make them feel more achievable. These incremental steps build confidence and momentum, making the overall goal seem less overwhelming.

↦ *Example*
If you're training for a marathon, start by running shorter distances and gradually increase the length as your endurance builds. Each completed run brings you closer to the final goal.

· Flexibility and Adaptation

Even the most well crafted routines need room for flexibility. Life will throw unexpected challenges your way — injuries, school, family obligations, or the occasional burnout. The important thing is not to be derailed by these moments. When I've had to miss a session due to injury or illness, I learned to adjust instead of feeling defeated.

A missed day doesn't mean failure; it's just an opportunity to adapt and keep going. Flexibility, after all, is a form of resilience, and resilience is what keeps you on the path.

For example, if your usual training time is disrupted, adapt by fitting in a shorter workout later in the day. If an injury prevents you from practicing certain techniques, focus on mental training or conditioning exercises instead. Flexibility keeps you moving forward, even when things don't go as planned.

Tracking, Reflecting, and Celebrating

Setting Benchmarks

To measure progress, set clear benchmarks. Make them specific and timebound, like, "I will increase my pushup count by 20% over the next month." Benchmarks give you a concrete way to assess your growth and stay motivated.

Tracking Progress

Use a journal, app, or even a simple checklist to track your practice sessions. Write down the exercises you completed, how you felt, and any milestones achieved. Reflect on your entries weekly or monthly — what's improving, what's still a struggle? By identifying these patterns, you can make informed adjustments. Maybe you need to focus more on endurance, or perhaps your flexibility is improving faster than expected. Tracking gives you a concrete sense of progress, which can be incredibly motivating.

Reflecting on Outcomes

Reflection is where the real growth happens. It's easy to get caught up in the grind of daily practice and miss the progress you're making. But when you take the time to reflect — whether by writing in a journal or simply reviewing your goals — you'll notice patterns of growth by looking at what's working and what isn't. Reflection helps you appreciate how far you've come and gives you the insight needed to finetune your approach, ensuring your efforts are always moving you closer to your goals.

Adjusting Your Routine

Based on your reflections, refine your routine. Perhaps it's time to increase the intensity, try a new technique, or devote more time to a particular skill. Just as a warrior continually sharpens their blade, you should continually hone your routine, making it sharper, more effective, and more aligned with your goals.

Celebrating Successes

Celebrate every win, no matter how small. Did you finally nail that difficult kata or form? Treat yourself to a favorite meal or a night out with friends. Did you stay consistent with your training for a full week? Take a rest day and enjoy the satisfaction of knowing you're building momentum. Small celebrations reinforce positive habits and keep motivation high. They remind you that progress, no matter how slow, is still progress.

Practical Tips for Maintaining Discipline and Routines

1. **Accountability**
   Accountability is key. Share your goals with a training partner or coach, and check in regularly to track your progress. Having someone to support and challenge you can make a significant difference in maintaining your discipline. Knowing that someone else is invested in your success adds an emotional layer of support, making it easier to stay committed when your motivation wavers.

2. **Mindfulness and Focus**
   Incorporate mindfulness practices like meditation or deep breathing into your routine. These techniques can enhance your focus and keep you mentally sharp during training. Starting or ending your training with a five-minute meditation or breathing exercise can sharpen your mental clarity, helping you approach each session with focus.

3. **Visual Aids**
   Use visual aids — apps like HabitBull or physical charts can give you a visual representation of your success, boosting your commitment to long-term growth.

4. **Reward Systems**
   Establish a reward system for yourself. Whether it's taking a rest day after a week of consistent practice or indulging in a favorite activity, rewards help reinforce your commitment.

5. **Community and Support**
   Engage with a community or support group that shares similar goals. Being part of a supportive community provides encouragement, inspiration, and accountability. Group activities or challenges can also make your routine more enjoyable.

Conclusion

Discipline and routines are your greatest allies in the journey toward mastery, inside and outside of practice. They provide the structure you need to keep moving forward, even when motivation wanes or the path becomes difficult. Remember, the path of mastery is a marathon, not a sprint; therefore, every small step you take brings you closer to becoming the best version of yourself. Stay patient, stay focused, and never forget to celebrate the progress you've made. The journey may be long, but with each day of disciplined practice, you are carving your path to success.

"We are what we repeatedly do. Excellence, then, is not an act, but a habit."

— Aristotle

Chapter 9: Building New Routines — Training for the U.S. Open ISKA World Martial Arts Championships

When I began training for the U.S. Open ISKA World Martial Arts Championships, I knew I needed to adjust my workout routine to focus on two crucial attributes for success in martial arts: speed and power. To achieve this, I targeted my core muscles and refined my breaking techniques by adjusting the height of my concrete blocks' resistance. These strategies proved pivotal in helping me perform at the highest level and break a world record (16 patio blocks) at the New England Regional Breaking Championships.

Strengthening the Core: Incorporating Cable Exercises

· Strategy

To develop the explosive speed and power essential for my martial arts techniques, I incorporated cable exercises into my workout routine. The core muscles play a central role in generating force and maintaining balance — two vital components of effective martial arts execution. Cable exercises allowed me to engage and strengthen my core more dynamically.

· Workout Routine

- **Progressive Loading:**
  I started each session with lighter weights to engage my core muscles and ensure proper form. As the sets progressed, I gradually increased the resistance to challenge my muscles more intensively. This method helped build a solid foundation and gradually enhanced my core's endurance and strength.

- **Reverse Pyramid Training:**
  After reaching the peak weight load, I would reverse the pyramid by working my way back down to lighter weights. This method not only tested my endurance but also pushed my core muscles to adapt to different resistance levels, boosting both my explosive power and muscle endurance.

· Physics in Action

The cable exercises were based on the principle of physics, particularly force, mass, and acceleration. By increasing the resistance and varying the load, I enhanced the power and speed of my movements, which translated directly into my martial arts techniques. Every punch, kick, or breaking strike relies on the proper generation of force, and strengthening the core allowed me to maximize my speed and power.

· Outcome

Incorporating cable exercises into my routine not only improved my core strength but also gave me the agility and power I needed to perform highspeed techniques with precision. This was a critical element of my preparation for the U.S. Open, allowing me to execute fast, powerful movements in competition.

Refining Techniques: Adjusting Block Height

· Challenge

While training for the U.S. Open, I recognized that to simulate competition conditions and refine my breaking techniques, I needed to adjust the height of my concrete blocks. Typically, breaking blocks are set on concrete blocks, but the concrete blocks add a base height that, combined with the blocks I wanted to break, resulted in a total height that was disadvantageous for me at my height. I needed to decrease the total height of the stacked blocks, but I couldn't take out the blocks I wanted to break; instead, I figured out that by lowering the base concrete blocks, I could achieve a lower overall structure height and break more effectively (see images at the end of this chapter). Lowering the block height presented a challenge, but it helped me finetune my stance, accuracy, and power generation.

Since I am short, lowering the height of the blocks effectively increases my height in relation to my stance. This adjustment improves balance, comfort, accessibility, and posture while allowing me to generate more power and speed from my hips.

Many tall competitors have attempted this method; however, due to their height, they fail to utilize their speed and power effectively, as they need to increase (rather than decrease) the height of the blocks.

· Solution

- **Using Patio Blocks As Stands:**
  To decrease the height of the concrete blocks, I used patio blocks as stands, reducing the height by about five to six inches. This forced me to modify my technique and adjust my stance, as I had to generate power from a slightly different angle, simulating the height and resistance I would face in competition.

- **Technique Refinement:**
  Training with the blocks at a lower height required me to focus on precision, accuracy, and generating power from the hips and legs. This refined my stance and overall breaking technique, helping me to execute my breaks with greater efficiency.

· Outcome

This modification to my breaking practice was instrumental in my preparation for the U.S. Open. By practicing with the decreased height, I was able to approach the actual breaking techniques with greater confidence and precision. The combination of enhanced core strength and refined technique ultimately contributed to my success in the U.S. Open ISKA World Martial Arts Championships and allowed me to achieve the world record (that is still held as of publishing) by breaking 16 concrete blocks at the New England Regional Breaking Championships in Uncasville, Connecticut, on August 3, 2008.

Conclusion

Training for the U.S. Open ISKA World Martial Arts Championships required not only physical conditioning but also thoughtful adjustments to my training routines. By focusing on core strength and refining my techniques, I was able to improve both my speed and power. These changes were key to breaking competition records and achieving success on one of the biggest stages in martial arts.

Whether preparing for a major competition or simply aiming for personal growth, adapting your training methods — incorporating core focused exercises and refining your techniques — can lead to significant improvements.

Training for a World Record

In 2005, I took on an extraordinary challenge — helping a colleague break the world record for the most boards broken in 60 seconds. This wasn't just about skill or strength; it was about pushing beyond physical and mental limits, overcoming past failures, and embracing a relentless drive to succeed. After multiple failed attempts, bruised hands, and battles with fatigue, we knew something had to change. A carefully crafted new routine turned a near impossible goal into a record breaking reality.

LB attempted the record four times with the International Sport Karate Association (ISKA). He tied the record in 2004 during the *Late Show with David Letterman*. In 2005, he asked me to train him. That year, both my arms were broken, and I wasn't competing. So, I took about six months to train him intensively. In the summer of 2005, we were invited (Team Bergamo Schick Quattro) to Hollywood, California, to break the record. He successfully broke the record — 487 boards. The record is recorded with the ISKA but not with the Guinness World Records.

Strength Training for Power and Speed

To ensure LB had the explosive power and speed necessary for breaking hundreds of boards in under a minute, I used my strength training routine but modified it to focus on building his physique, core strength, and muscle endurance.

· Strength Training Routine (3x per Week, 2-Hour Sessions)

- Weight Lifting for Explosive Power
- Core Strengthening for Speed & Stability
- Speed and Agility Drills

Building Stamina: Sprint Training

Stamina had always been the Achilles' heel in my colleague's previous attempts. Each time, he would start strong but fade by the end, watching the record slip through his fingers. He was determined, but determination alone wasn't enough — we needed a new approach. His frustration was palpable, and the stakes were high. It wasn't just about beating a number; it was about conquering the limits of his body and mind.

· The New Routine

We started with a two mile jog every day. Then we added a sprint training regimen on a baseball field, designed to simulate the explosive energy required during the 60second record attempt. The idea was simple but brutal — sprint 100 feet at full speed, then walk back to the starting point for recovery. This interval training taxed his cardiovascular system, teaching his body to recover quickly and maintain high energy output over time. It was designed to mimic the intense bursts of power he'd need while breaking boards, ensuring he could maintain peak performance through the entire minute.

· The Outcome

The sprint training was transformative. For the first time, he didn't run out of gas during a practice attempt. The fatigue that had once crippled his efforts was now manageable, and with each session, his confidence grew. No longer did he fear reaching the final seconds of the attempt — he knew his body was conditioned to handle it.

This newfound stamina was the turning point, the edge he needed to push past his previous limits and break through to a new level of performance.

Conditioning the Hands: Hammer Fist Training

In every previous attempt, his hands were his greatest weakness. By the end, they were swollen and bruised, looking like ground meat. The pain was unbearable, and it wasn't just the boards that became obstacles — it was his own body. We knew that if he didn't strengthen his hands, he would face the same outcome again. That's wh en we turned to hammer fist training, focusing on toughening not just the muscles, but the skin, bones, and tendons that would be tested in the record breaking attempt.

· The New Routine

I introduced hammer fist training, where he would eventually perform 300 hammer fists on a cinder block every day. This exercise was designed to toughen the skin, bones, and muscles in his hands, allowing them to adapt to the repeated impact of hitting solid surfaces.

· Gradual Adaptation

We started small, with just a few hammer fists a day. At first, it was painful — each strike sent shockwaves through his hands. But we knew that pushing too hard too fast could lead to injury, so we built up gradually. With each day, his hands became stronger and more resilient, adapting to the increasing demands. By the time we reached 300 hammer fists daily, his hands were no longer a liability — they had become weapons, capable of withstanding the punishment of breaking board after board.

· The Outcome

The hammer fist training toughened his hands, significantly reducing the damage they endured during the record attempt. His hands were now capable of striking with full force without fear of injury. This conditioning was crucial to his ability to break the boards effectively.

The Record-Breaking Success

The day of the record attempt felt different. There was an air of quiet confidence about him — he knew his body was ready, and his mind was focused. As the clock started, every strike was calculated, every movement precise. Unlike his previous attempts, there was no sign of fatigue as the seconds ticked away. His hands, conditioned through months of training, were relentless. When the final 487th board splintered under his strike and the clock stopped, he had done it. He had broken the world record, shattering not just the boards but the mental and physical barriers that had held him back for so long. It was a moment of triumph, not just for him, but for everyone who had watched his journey from frustration to success.

This record breaking success was the result of months of discipline, perseverance, and carefully designed routines. It's a testament to what's possible when you commit fully to a goal and push beyond your limits. Whether you're training for your own personal achievement or striving for greatness in any area of life, remember — success isn't about luck or talent alone. It's about building the right routines, sticking to them, and having the patience to see them through. Just like my colleague, with the right plan and determination, you too can break through your barriers and set new records of your own.

July 2005 – Hollywood, California: Black Belt Magazine's Festival of Martial Arts. Multiple pine boards (1″ x 10″ x 12″) per station, spaced using carpenter pencils, set on 120 concrete stands. Total blocks set up: 500. Record achieved: 487.

Raphael Vélez is in the front holding a timer in this video.www.youtube.com/watch?v=gRFnum0FKAA

July 2005 – Hollywood, California: Black Belt Magazine's Festival of Martial Arts. LB mentally prepares to smash 500 boards in 50 seconds.

Sixteen patio blocks (2" x 8" x 15") are set up on two additional patio blocks to reduce the overall height of the stack.

2008 – Raphael Vélez at Mohegan Sun Casino & Resort, Uncasville, Connecticut, competing in the New England Regional Breaking Championships and setting a world record by breaking 15 patio blocks.

"The difference between the impossible and the possible lies in a person's determination."
— Tommy Lasorda

Chapter 10: Measuring Results

Measuring progress is more than a technical exercise — it's a journey of self discovery and growth. In martial arts and in life, it's easy to lose sight of how far you've come when you're focused on daily routines. But by regularly assessing your development, you not only sharpen your skills but also gain insight into your personal evolution. Each step forward, no matter how small, brings you closer to mastering your craft and yourself. This chapter explores how to measure your results effectively, helping you stay motivated, accountable, and always moving toward your goals.

The Importance of Measuring Results: Accountability, Motivation, and Growth

Tracking your progress does more than just hold you accountable — it gives each training session purpose. Imagine how discouraging it can feel when your efforts seem to yield no results. But by measuring your progress, you can see the small victories that accumulate over time. For example, when I was working on improving my speed, tracking my sprint times helped me realize I was consistently shaving seconds off each run — even when I didn't feel any faster. Those small improvements, when recognized, kept me motivated to push forward on days when progress felt slow.

Regular measurement also allows you to identify both your strengths and areas for improvement. With this self-awareness, you can tailor your training to maintain balance and avoid plateaus. Importantly, tracking results ensures your goals remain flexible and realistic. By reflecting on your progress, you can adjust your objectives to stay challenged without becoming overwhelmed or frustrated.

Motivational Insight

Think of tracking progress like climbing a staircase. Each step forward might feel small, but over time, those small steps add up to significant gains. Keep your focus on the next step, and you'll be surprised at how far you've climbed.

Methods for Measuring Progress and Refining Techniques

1. **Video Recording and Analysis**
   Video recording is one of the most powerful tools for measuring progress because it provides a tangible way to see how far you've come. Sometimes what feels correct in the moment doesn't always look that way on video. I remember a time when I thought my strikes were perfectly aligned, but after reviewing the footage, I noticed subtle flaws in my form that were robbing me of power. The realization was humbling, but it also gave me clear direction for improvement. The emotional impact of seeing yourself grow on video over time is profound — it's a visual reminder of your hard work and dedication.

   When analyzing the footage, pay close attention to key areas like:

   a. **Stance and Technique:** Is your foot placement and body alignment consistent? Are your movements fluid and precise?
   b. **Breaking Success:** Review the power, speed, and accuracy of your strikes. Often, what feels powerful in the moment may not look as effective on video, revealing areas for improvement.

   ↦ *Personal Anecdote*
   I once thought I'd nailed a complex breaking technique, only to notice on video that my stance was slightly off, causing a loss of power in my strike. This realization led me to focus on my footwork for the next few weeks, resulting in a major improvement during my next competition.

   ↦ *Takeaway*
   Regular video analysis allows for incremental improvements that add up over time. It's not just about recording — it's about reviewing, reflecting, and refining.

2. **Benchmarking: Learning from the Best and the Worst**
   Benchmarking is more than simply comparing yourself to others; it's about learning from both their strengths and weaknesses by analyzing their performance. When you study top performers,

96

you're not just looking at their technical abilities — you're absorbing their mindset, their discipline, and their approach to the craft. Equally valuable is learning from those who've struggled.

Early in my journey, I realized that watching someone fail at a technique I was struggling with showed me exactly what to avoid. It gave me a new perspective and renewed confidence that I could overcome the same hurdle. Benchmarking offers powerful lessons in both success and failure.

↦ *Personal Anecdote*
While struggling with a specific breaking technique, I initially focused on the best breakers for inspiration. However, it wasn't until I studied someone who failed at the same technique that I realized what I was doing wrong. Avoiding their mistakes helped me master the move, boosting my confidence in the process.

↦ *Takeaway*
Benchmarking offers a dual perspective — learning from excellence and avoiding pitfalls. Both are invaluable for refining your technique.

Practical Tools for Tracking Progress

1. **Journaling**
   A training journal is more than just a log of your sessions — it's a personal roadmap of your journey. Each entry captures a moment in time, recording not only what you did but how you felt. Over weeks and months, these small notes accumulate into a powerful record of your growth. I often look back at my journals from years ago and marvel at how far I've come. What once felt like an insurmountable challenge is now part of my daily practice. Journaling doesn't just track progress — it reminds you of the resilience and dedication that carried you through each challenge.

   ↦ *Example*
   "August 5th: Focused on roundhouse kicks. Notice better balance and stability compared to last week" Regular entries like this reveal patterns, breakthroughs, and areas that need attention.

2. Progress Photos and Videos

A picture is worth a thousand words, and video is worth even more. Visual documentation of your form over time can reveal subtle improvements that aren't always noticeable in daily training.

↦ *Example*
Record yourself sparring at regular intervals — perhaps monthly — and review the footage to track improvements in form, speed, and technique. This visual feedback can be a powerful motivator.

3. Performance Metrics

Numbers offer concrete evidence of progress, whether you're tracking strength, speed, or technique execution. For instance, you might track the number of pushups, punches, or kicks you can perform in a minute and aim to increase that number over time. Performance metrics offer a clear, objective way to measure growth and provide a sense of accomplishment each time you surpass your previous best.

↦ *Example*
If you're working on endurance, note the time it takes to complete a set distance or the number of rounds you can spar before feeling fatigued. Over time, aim to improve these metrics, providing concrete evidence of your improvement.

4. Benchmark Tests

Regularly conducting fitness or technique tests allows you to assess your growth in a structured way. These tests should be consistent so that comparisons are accurate.

↦ *Example*
Perform a benchmark test every three months, assessing core exercises like sit-ups, pushups, and running. Comparing results over time will clearly show how much you've improved and where you need to focus.

5. **Feedback from Instructors**

   Feedback from instructors, coaches, and teammates is invaluable because they see things you might be too close to notice. I remember a time when I thought I had perfected a certain strike, only for my teammate to point out a subtle flaw in my stance's alignment that was limiting my power. It was a small correction, but it completely transformed the effectiveness of my strikes. Feedback isn't just about fixing mistakes — it's about unlocking your potential and helping you reach levels you didn't think were possible. The guidance of an experienced eye can make all the difference in your progress.

   ↦ *Example*
   After a sparring session, ask for specific feedback on your technique and strategy. Incorporating other's insights into your training can significantly enhance your progress.

6. **Digital Tools and Apps**

   In today's digital age, a wide range of tools and apps can help track and analyze your progress. From fitness apps that log workouts to those that monitor heart rates, these tools provide clear visual data that can help you stay on track.

   ↦ *Example*
   Use a fitness app to record your workout sessions, track progress in real time, and see visual charts of your improvement.

Reflecting on Progress and Adjusting Training Plans

1. **Regular Reflection**

   Reflection is where you see the real fruits of your labor. On the tough days, when progress feels painfully slow, looking back at where you started can reignite your motivation. Those early journal entries, video clips, or performance metrics remind you that even small, incremental progress is still progress. Reflection gives you the power to acknowledge your growth, understand where you need to improve, and adjust your training with intention. It's about celebrating the journey, not just the destination, and ensuring each step forward is guided by purpose.

↦ *Motivational Insight*
Progress can sometimes feel slow day to day, but reflecting on your journey shows just how much you've grown over time.

2. **Celebrating Milestones**
   Celebrate every milestone, no matter how small. Whether it's improving a technique or hitting a personal best, acknowledging these wins keeps you motivated and engaged.

   ↦ *Example*
   After hitting a new personal best in pushups, treat yourself to something special — maybe a new piece of training gear or a day off to relax.

3. **Adjusting Your Training Plan**
   Adjusting your training plan isn't a sign of failure — it's a mark of growth and resilience. As you progress, what worked before might no longer be enough to challenge you, and that's a good thing. It means you're improving. I've often found that making small tweaks — whether it's increasing the intensity of a drill or focusing on a different technique — has reignited my passion for training. These adjustments keep the journey fresh and ensure you continue moving forward, avoiding plateaus and keeping your progress on track.

   ↦ *Example*
   If your stamina isn't improving as quickly as you'd like, incorporate more cardio sessions like interval sprints or long distance runs to challenge your muscles in a new way.

Conclusion: Measuring Progress, Celebrating Growth

Measuring progress is more than just data points — it's the story of your journey toward mastery. Every benchmark, every video analysis, every journal entry is a testament to your dedication and growth. As you continue measuring and reflecting on your progress, remember it's not about perfection. It's about celebrating the small wins, learning from setbacks, and always moving forward. Each step, no matter how small, builds the foundation for your future success. Keep tracking, keep refining, and most importantly, keep believing in your ability to achieve greatness.

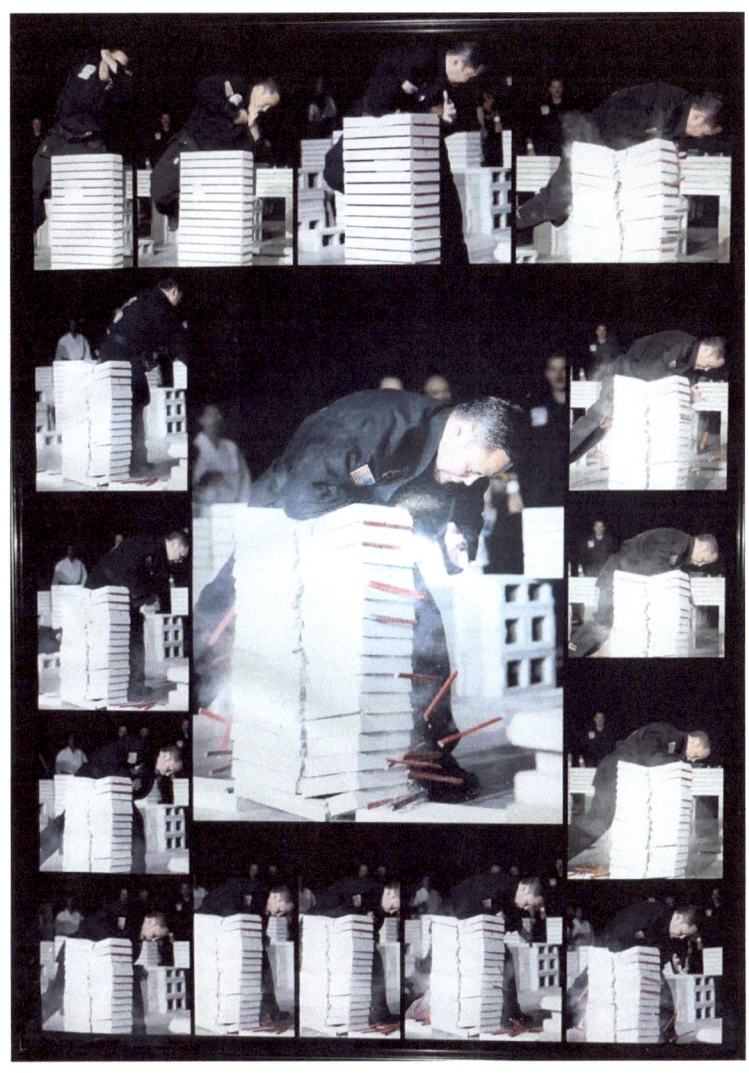

In this photo, GM Vélez demonstrates his world record 15 patio break, step by step.

"Without continual growth and progress, such words as improvement, achievement, and success have no meaning."
— Benjamin Franklin

Chapter 11: Real World Mindsets: Lessons from World Champion Martial Artists

In the world of martial arts, champions are not only made through physical training but through the cultivation of a resilient mindset. Mental toughness, discipline, and a strong sense of purpose drive worldclass athletes to push past their limits and continually evolve. This chapter delves into the mindset of two martial arts champions and personal friends of mine, Fernando Camareno and Mike Thomas, exploring how their mental strategies have shaped their journeys and contributed to their incredible success.

Through their stories, you will see the principle I share with you in action. Their experiences demonstrate the journey toward mastery is as much mental as it is physical and how a champion's mindset can inspire and uplift others. As you read their stories, I hope you can envision yourself as a champion. You can be a champion, too.

"Real world mindsets don't fold under pressure. They adapt, they endure, and they finish what they start."

~Unknown

Fernando Camareno: The Power of Focus and Resilience

Fernando Camareno with 2005 USBA/WBA Breaker of the Year Awards.

Fernando Camareno is a highly respected martial artist, recognized for his contributions to both martial arts and fitness. He is a multiple time world champion and world record holder who has shaped his life and career through the strength of his mindset. From overcoming personal loss to returning to competitive form after a near death experience, Camareno's journey offers a testament to the power of mental resilience and visualization.

Building the Mindset of a Champion

At just eight years old, Camareno experienced a pivotal moment that would set the foundation for his champion mindset. A world champion in kickboxing, Benny "The Jet" Urquidez put his belt around young Fernando's waist and said, "If you learn to focus on life and follow the directions of the people who love you, you can achieve what you set out to do — even becoming a world champion." This experience planted a seed of belief in Camareno, reinforcing the idea that hearing positive, empowering words can fuel your growth and drive.

That simple statement became a mental anchor for Camareno, helping him push through early setbacks. He recalls losing 13 consecutive competitions at the start of his martial arts career, but he reframed these losses through the advice of a mentor: "A winner isn't someone who always wins, but someone who gets tired of losing and decides to change." This mindset shift empowered Camareno to keep competing, eventually leading him to years of consecutive victories.

Overcoming Life's Greatest Challenges

Camareno's resilience was tested again when he was arranging a ladder in the middle of a job. He encountered some high voltage cables and received a shock of 13,570 volts, suffering a life threatening electrical accident. This left him severely injured, with second and third degree burns, muscle atrophy, and limited mobility. While most people might have given up, Camareno found strength in his faith and reconnected with his goal to compete.

After years of recovery, he joined Team Bergamo Schick Quattro, the group he had admired for their world records in breaking competitions. This opportunity reignited his competitive spirit, and at the age of 38, he qualified for his first world championship. From 2004 to 2009, Fernando Camareno won seven world championships and set six world records in breaking.

Key Takeaways from Camareno's Mindset

- **Focus on Positive Reinforcement:**
  Early encouragement can ignite long lasting motivation.
- **Learn from Loss:**
  Every failure is a step toward success, provided you analyze and adjust.
- **Never Give Up:**
  Age, setbacks, and physical limitations are surmountable when your mind is aligned with your goals.
- **Mental Strength:**
  Mental preparation and perseverance are as important as physical ability when pursuing greatness.

If you are interested in learning more about Fernando Camareno and his story, visit his website: *Mastergroup.my.canva.site/mastercamarenocoach*

Mike Thomas: Mental Resilience Through Adversity

Mike Thomas with the 2020 USBA/WBA Champion belt and a sanctioned record of breaking 47 out of 50 patio blocks in 10 seconds using a palm strike.

Mike Thomas, another martial arts champion, is known for his strategic approach to both competition and life. His mindset was shaped by early hardships, personal tragedy, and the determination to keep moving forward in the face of challenges. Much like Camareno, Thomas found strength in resilience and a deep belief in the power of mental preparation.

A Champion's Core Beliefs

For Thomas, the fusion of purpose and passion is what creates a world champion. He credits his instructor, Master Charles Edwards, for instilling in him the belief that anything worth achieving requires hard work, sacrifice, and perseverance. Thomas also believes that helping others achieve their goals enhances your own journey. He explains, "Motivating and teaching someone else will help keep you focused on your own goals, even when it doesn't seem possible."

Overcoming Physical and Mental Challenges

Thomas' mindset has been tested multiple times. At 23, while preparing for his black belt in Tae Kwon Do, he suffered a severe knee injury, tearing his anterior cruciate ligament (ACL) and medial collateral ligament (MCL). Despite the injury, he rehabilitated himself, passed his black belt test, and underwent surgery — afterward.

In 2024, another life altering challenge arose when Thomas suffered a seizure that left him in a medically induced coma for 11 days and in the hospital for 21 days. With the loss of 30 pounds, strength, and motor skills, many IV lines, and a deep vein thrombosis (DVT) blood clot, the recovery process was grueling. Although advised by doctors to stop practicing martial arts, Thomas' mindset remains unshaken. He adapted his training and believes this setback is temporary. "Where the mind goes, the body will follow — for better or worse," he reflects.

Key Takeaways from Thomas' Mindset

- **Mental Conditioning Is Key**
  Just as important as physical training, a strong mind guides the body through adversity.
- **Adaptability:**
  Facing physical limitations doesn't mean giving up — it means finding new ways to train and stay motivated.
- **Purpose Driven Training:**
  Having a strong "why" behind your goals ensures you stay focused even through the toughest challenges.
- **Embrace Mentorship and Support:**
  Success is rarely achieved alone; finding the right mentors and community is essential.
- **Mind Over Matter:**
  Push past the mental barriers that limit your potential — what feels like the end is often just the beginning.

Lessons from Two Champions: Key Themes for Success

Both Camareno and Thomas share mental strategies that have shaped their paths to success. Here are some key themes to apply to your own martial arts journey:

1. **Visualization and Goal Setting**
   Both champions emphasize the importance of visualizing success. Seeing yourself achieve your goals, whether in competition or personal growth, helps you stay on track and motivated.

2. **Resilience in the Face of Setbacks**
   Adversity is inevitable, but how you respond to it is what matters. Both martial artists learned to use personal tragedies and failures as stepping stones to growth.

3. **The Power of a Strong "Why"**
   Knowing why you're pursuing your goals keeps you motivated through difficult times. For both Camareno and Thomas, their "why" gave them the resilience to continue in the face of adversity.

4. **Discipline and Routine**
   Consistent training is a hallmark of both champions' journeys. But they also stress the importance of adaptability — adjusting your routine when necessary ensures continuous growth.

5. **Community and Mentorship**
   Both martial artists attribute much of their success to the mentors and communities that supported them. Surrounding yourself with likeminded people who share your vision is critical for growth.

Conclusion: Cultivating the Champion's Mindset

The journeys of Fernando Camareno and Mike Thomas illustrate the importance of mindset in achieving success, both in their training and throughout their personal lives. Their stories show us that mental resilience, discipline, and the drive to help others are fundamental components of the champion's mindset.

As you progress on your own martial arts journey, remember these key lessons:

- **Stay focused** on your goals, even when challenges arise.
- **Visualize your success** and embrace the process of growth.
- **Surround yourself** with a supportive community that believes in your potential.

Whether you're just beginning your journey or striving to reach the next level, the stories of Camareno and Thomas serve as powerful reminders that with the right mindset, anything is possible.

"He who is not courageous enough to take risks will accomplish nothing in life".
— Muhammad Ali

Chapter 12: Sample Workout Routines and Conditioning Resources

This appendix provides a comprehensive set of workout routines, traditional martial arts drills, and conditioning exercises designed to enhance your training. Whether you're looking to build strength, improve endurance, or address specific behavioral challenges, these resources offer a variety of tools to support your progress.

My Personal Workout Routines

In my training, I follow the pyramid principle, which involves progressively increasing the weight with each set, reaching your peak at the fourth or fifth set, then reducing the weight as you finish. This method allows for a combination of strength building and endurance, ensuring muscles are fully engaged throughout the workout. The goal is to push your body while avoiding injury, giving your muscles time to adapt and grow.

The pyramid principle is designed to engage your muscles through a wide range of weights. Starting with lighter weights, you warm up the muscles and prepare them for heavier loads. As the weight increases, you challenge your muscles to build strength. Reducing the weight toward the end helps reinforce endurance and muscle memory. This method prevents your muscles from adapting to a specific weight, encouraging continuous development.

· Hammer Grip Dumbbell Press Routine

One of my favorite chest exercises is the hammer grip dumbbell press, which targets multiple muscle groups at once. This exercise not only engages the pectoralis major (your main chest muscle) but also the anterior deltoids (front of the shoulders) and triceps, making it a powerful all-in-one upper body movement.

Incline hammer grip dumbbell press is next in my routine, targeting the upper portion of the chest. I make sure to change the angle of the incline bench with each set to ensure I'm working every angle of the chest muscles. For a strong pump, I typically aim for 10-15 reps per set. The constant variation in angles helps stimulate muscle growth and prevents adaptation.

Following that, I move on to the hammer grip decline dumbbell press to emphasize the lower chest. The combination of flat, incline, and decline presses ensures I engage the entire pectoral muscle group for well rounded development.

Next, I perform chest flys on the machine. This exercise isolates the chest muscles, allowing for a deep stretch and contraction at the top of the movement. To finish, I incorporate dumbbell pullovers, which activate not just the chest but also the latissimus dorsi (upper back) and help improve overall upper body flexibility.

↦ *Summary of Benefits*
This chest routine is ideal for martial artists who want to build upper body strength and endurance, supporting powerful strikes and increased stability during sparring and breaking.

· Alternating Workouts for Continuous Gains

Alternating between dumbbells and barbells ensures varied muscle engagement, reducing the risk of plateauing. To keep my muscles guessing, I alternate between using hammer grip dumbbells one week and a barbell the next. This variation in grip and equipment forces my muscles to engage in new ways, promoting both muscle mass and strength gains. For example, one week my chest routine might center around dumbbells, and the following week, I'll switch to barbells. This keeps my workout fresh and prevents my muscles from adapting to the same exercises, which is essential for continued growth.

· Changing Up the Routine Every Three to Five Weeks

One of the most important aspects of my training philosophy is constantly changing my workout routine every three to five weeks. By switching up exercises, angles, and rep schemes, you ensure your muscles are continually challenged, promoting growth and preventing stagnancy. This constant adaptation helps maintain steady gains in strength, size, and endurance. For example, I might focus on my back and chest one day, shoulders and arms the next, and legs on the third day. I never let my routine become stale.

· Leg Workout Routine

My leg workout is the longest session in my training plan, and I like to start with a single leg extension. I alternate each leg, beginning with lightweight until I can no longer perform another rep. Then, I add both legs and increase the weight, pushing myself until failure, before returning to lighter weights again. This method keeps the muscles engaged and active, effectively increasing both strength and endurance. This method usually consists of 10 sets of leg extensions, giving me a thorough workout. By alternating between single leg and two leg exercises, I ensure both sides of the body develop equally and that my legs receive a comprehensive workout.

· Pre-Exhaust Method

I also like to use the pre-exhaust method during my leg and chest training. This method involves performing high intensity exercises at the beginning of a session to fatigue the muscles before moving on to heavier resistance training. By exhausting the muscles early on, I ensure I get the most out of the resistance exercises that follow, maximizing muscle engagement.

For instance, I might begin a leg workout with leg extensions to pre-exhaust the quadriceps, then move on to squats or leg presses. This ensures I push my muscles to their limit, leading to better results in both strength and muscle development.

Consistency, Dedication, and Creativity

Consistency and dedication have always been the pillars of my workout success. I worked long and hard to achieve the results I wanted, but the key to my progress has been creativity and willingness to change up my routine. Being creative with your exercise routine keeps it enjoyable and helps avoid burnout while also keeping your body in a state of constant adaptation and improvement.

Rest and Recovery

After each intense workout, it's crucial to give your muscles time to recover. Make sure to stretch after every session to reduce stiffness and soreness. Incorporating at least one rest day per week, or alternating muscle groups, ensures your body has enough time to rebuild muscle fibers stronger than before.

Workout Routine

You can modify this based on your personal fitness level.

· Chest Routine (Pyramid Principle)

1. **Barbell Bench Press:** 8 sets (using the pyramid principle: light to heavy, then back to light)
   a. Example: Start light, increase the weight with each set, and then reduce back to the initial weight (45, 135, 225, 315, 345, 225, 135, 45 pounds)
2. **Hammer Grip Dumbbell Press:** 4 sets of 6-15 reps
   a. Alternate between dumbbells and barbells weekly.
3. **Hammer Grip Incline Dumbbell Press:** 4 sets of 6-15 reps
   a. Change the bench angle for each set to target different parts of the chest
4. **Hammer Grip Decline Dumbbell Press:** 4 sets of 6-15 reps
5. **Chest Flys (machine):** 4 sets of 6-15 reps
6. **Dumbbell Pullovers:** 3 sets of 6-15 reps (perform on an incline, flat, and decline)

· Leg Routine

1. **Single Leg Extensions:** 10 sets of 6-12 reps
   a. Start light, increase gradually, then return to the starting weight
2. **Leg Press (45degree angle):** 4 sets of 6-15 reps
3. **Leg Press (90degree angle):** 4 sets of 6-15 reps
4. **Vertical Leg Press (Smith machine):** 4 sets of 6-15 reps
5. **Squat Machine:** 4 sets of 6-15 reps

6. **Hack Squat Machine:** 4 sets of 6-15 reps
7. **Leg Curl Machine:** 4 sets of 6-15 reps
8. **Decline Dumbbell Leg Curls (on sit-up bench):** 4 sets of 6-15 reps
9. **Lunges:** 4 sets of 12 reps per leg

· **Back & Triceps Routine**

This routine targets the back and triceps, building upper body strength and stability.

1. **Close Grip Lat Pulldown:** 4 sets of 6-15 reps
2. **Wide Grip Lat Pulldown:** 4 sets of 6-15 reps
3. **Close Grip Pulldown (back):** 4 sets of 6-15 reps
4. **Wide Grip Pulldown (back):** 4 sets of 6-15 reps
5. **Seated Row (wide grip and close grip):** 4 sets of 6-15 reps
6. **Smith Machine Bent Over Row:** 4 sets of 6-15 reps
7. **Single Arm Dumbbell Row:** 4 sets of 6-15 reps per arm
8. **Decline Bench Pullover (dumbbell or barbell):** 4 sets of 6-15 reps
9. **Cable Overhead Triceps Extension:** 4 sets of 6-15 reps
10. **Triceps Extension (front and reverse grip):** 4 sets of 6-15 reps
11. **Skull Crushers:** 3 sets of 6-15 reps
12. **Overhead Triceps Extensions:** 3 sets of 6-15 reps
13. **Reverse Grip Triceps Bench Press:** 4 sets of 6-15 reps

· **Bicep & Shoulder Routine**

A combined routine for biceps and shoulders, enhancing upper body strength and muscle definition.

1. **Smith Machine Front Shoulder Press** 4 sets of 6-15 reps
2. **EZ Curl Bar Biceps Curl 21s:** 3 sets
    a. Tip: 21s involve 7 reps of the lower half, 7 of the upper half, and 7 full curls. Alternate the angle each set.
3. **Hammer Grip Alternating Dumbbell Curls:** 4 sets of 6-15 reps
4. **Seated Bicep Curls (with back support):** 4 sets of 6-15 reps
5. **Concentration Bicep Curl:** 4 sets of 10-15 reps

6. **Dumbbell Pullover (incline position):** 4 sets of 6-15 reps
7. **Dumbbell Lateral Raise:** 4 sets of 6-15 reps
8. **Seated Rear Delt Fly:** 4 sets of 6-15 reps
9. **Single Arm Dumbbell Raises (using a sit-up bench, lying incline position):** 4 sets of 6-15 reps

· **Chest & Bicep Routine**

1. **Barbell Bench Press** 6 sets of 4-15 reps
2. **EZ Curl Bar Biceps Curl 21s** 3 sets each of 7 reps (total 21)
   a. Tip: Involve 7 reps of the lower half, 7 of the upper half, and 7 full curls
3. **Hammer Grip Dumbbell Press** 4 sets of 8-10 reps
4. **Hammer Grip Alternating Dumbbell Curls** 4 sets of 10-12 reps
5. **Hammer Grip Dumbbell Incline Press** 4 sets of 8-10 reps
6. **Seated Bicep Curls (with back support)** 4 sets of 10-12 reps
7. **Hammer Grip Decline Dumbbell Press** 4 sets of 8-10 reps
8. **Concentration Bicep Curl** 4 sets of 10-12 reps
9. **Chest Fly on Machine** 4 sets of 8-10 reps
10. **Dumbbell Pullover (incline position)** 4 sets of 12-15 reps

· **Light Cardio Routines**

Light cardio exercises are low intensity activities that gently elevate the heart rate without putting excessive strain on the body. Here are some great examples:

- **Brisk Walking:** A steady paced walk indoors or outdoors.
- **Treadmill Walking:** Set at a low incline for slight resistance.
- **Walking in Place:** Great for warmups or limited space.

Core Routines

A core routine is a structured set of exercises designed to strengthen the core muscles, which include the abdominals, obliques, lower back, and deep stabilizing muscles like the transverse abdominis. These muscles provide stability, balance, and power for daily movements, sports, and athletic performance.

Here are some core routines tailored for different fitness levels and goals:

· Beginner Core Routine

Great for beginners, injury recovery, or warmups, these low impact exercises build on foundational strength.

1. **Pelvic Tilts:** 3 sets of 10 reps
2. **Seated Knee Lifts:** 3 sets of 12 reps
3. **Glute Bridges:** 3 sets of 12 reps
4. **Bird Dog:** 3 sets of 10 reps per side

· Intermediate Core Routine

Ideal for overall core strengthening, functional movement, and increased stability and balance.

1. **Plank (Forearm or High Plank):** 3 sets of 30-45 seconds
2. **Bicycle Crunches:** 3 sets of 15 reps per side
3. **Russian Twists:** 3 sets of 20 reps (10 per side)
4. **Leg Raises:** 3 sets of 12 reps
5. **Superman Hold:** 3 sets of 30 seconds

· Advanced Core Routine

These high intensity exercises are best for athletes, martial artists, and advanced fitness enthusiasts to further increase strength and endurance.

1. **Hanging Leg Raises:** 3 sets of 12 reps
2. **Ab Wheel Rollouts:** 3 sets of 10 reps
3. **VUps:** 3 sets of 15 reps
4. **Plank with Shoulder Taps:** 3 sets of 20 reps (10 per side)
5. **Dragon Flags:** 3 sets of 8 reps

· Sport Specific Core Routine

Perfect for martial artists, boxers, and athletes needing rotational power to build explosive strength and increase rotation.

1. **Medicine Ball Rotational Slams:** 3 sets of 12 reps
2. **Cable Woodchoppers:** 3 sets of 10 reps per side
3. **Hollow Body Hold:** 3 sets of 30 seconds
4. **Kettlebell Windmills:** 3 sets of 10 reps per side
5. **Plank to Explosive Knee Drive:** 3 sets of 12 reps per leg

Active Recovery

Active recovery is a low intensity movement or exercise performed on rest days or after intense workouts to promote muscle recovery, reduce soreness, and improve circulation without causing further strain on the body. Unlike complete rest, active recovery keeps the body moving at a light intensity to aid in faster healing and mobility.

Examples of active recovery include swimming at a relaxed pace, yoga, dynamic stretching, tai chi, and massage.

Example: Weekly Training Schedule

- **Monday:** chest routine, bicep & shoulder routine, and abs
- **Tuesday:** leg routine
- **Wednesday:** rest or light cardio and abs
- **Thursday:** back & triceps routine
- **Friday:** bicep & shoulder routine, core routine, and abs
- **Saturday:** light cardio or active recovery
- **Sunday:** rest day

Conclusion

By alternating exercises, changing routines every few weeks, and incorporating techniques like the pre-exhaust method, I ensure my body is constantly challenged. This variety is what keeps my muscles growing and my motivation high. If you're consistent, creative, and willing to push your limits, you'll see the gains you're working for.

"Champions keep playing until they get it right."

— Billie Jean King

Chapter 13: Traditional "Old School" Drills

Traditional "old school" drills have been the backbone of martial arts training for generations, designed to build both physical strength and mental toughness. These drills were fundamental in building the physical and mental toughness necessary for high level competition and often focus on building fundamental skills, conditioning the body, and instilling discipline and perseverance in practitioners. Over the years, I've practiced these drills on myself and my students, combining the wisdom of the master's with my own experience to sharpen both the body and mind. Consistency was key, and while the journey was long, the rewards were immense.

In this section, I'll delve into some old school drills I practiced on myself and my students to sharpen both body and mind. I constantly explored new training methods, but I also had the privilege of learning from the masters. By studying their techniques and body movements in person or through videotape, I gained valuable insights over the years, with consistency the major takeaway. These drills emphasize foundational martial arts skills, combining physical conditioning with technique development. Here are some examples of traditional drills I relied on, many of which are staples in martial arts training:

Kata/Hyung/Forms

In many traditional martial arts, kata (or forms) are prearranged sequences of movements that simulate various combat scenarios. While some martial arts disciplines do not incorporate katas, viewing them as unnecessary, I believe in their significance and the value they bring to practice. Forms training enhances coordination, muscle memory, balance, precision, and concentration, while also preserving the traditional techniques and principles passed down through generations.

I've personally trained in weapon katas, including the katana, nunchaku, escrima sticks, bo, and dagger, all of which have helped me develop my fighting spirit and rhythm. Focus on technical precision and smooth transitions between movements for maximum benefit.

Weapon Training

Training with traditional martial arts weapons such as swords, staffs, or nunchaku emphasizes weapon handling skills, coordination, and timing. Weapon drills not only enhance your martial arts abilities but also preserve the traditional techniques and principles that define the art form.

Start with lighter weapons to develop control before progressing to heavier ones. Mastering light weapons first allows for better understanding of balance and precision.

↦ *Examples*

- **Double Nunchaku Practice:** Working with two nunchaku builds ambidexterity and coordination.

- **Sword Training (katana/bo/escrima):** Focus on strikes, blocks, and fluid transitions to improve both offensive and defensive techniques.

GM Vélez practicing with double nunchaku.

GM Vélez, a member of the USA Kummooyeh Federation, practicing with a sword.

GM Vélez Performing a bo form.

Elizabeth and Nic practicing with a sword.

· Pad Work

Pad work is a staple in martial arts, emphasizing speed, power, and accuracy through striking drills. This training includes punches, kicks, knee strikes, elbow strikes, and palm strikes, all performed against a padded target to maximize impact while minimizing injury. Working with a partner provides real time feedback on technique and power, ensuring you continually refine your skills.

- **Purpose:** Emphasizes speed, power, and accuracy in striking combinations.
- **Techniques:** Punches, palm strikes, elbow strikes, knees, round kicks, side kicks, front kicks, and chops.
- **Tip:** Work with a partner who can provide immediate feedback on technique and power. Focus on proper form, then increase speed and intensity.

· Bag Work

Punching and kicking heavy bags or speed bags is a powerful drill for developing power, speed, and endurance. It's used in various martial arts, including boxing, karate, Muay Thai, and kickboxing. In my classes, I incorporated short rounds of bag work, including a variety of strikes — punches, kicks, knees, elbows, chops, and palm strikes.

1989 – Raphael Vélez practicing a flying kick on a heavy bag.

- **Purpose:** Develops power, speed, and endurance through striking.
- **Tip:** Vary your combinations regularly to challenge different muscle groups and avoid monotony. Rotate between punches, kicks, and elbows to target different muscle groups.

· Makiwara Training

Common in traditional karate, makiwara training involves striking a padded target to develop power, accuracy, and condition the muscles, bones, knuckles, palm, elbow, and striking surfaces. This helped me build stamina and endurance. While the makiwara and heavy bag are both excellent tools for training in the martial arts, the makiwara is organically superior for martial arts training. However, in my view, the main purpose of makiwara training is learning how to generate power effectively.

- **Purpose:** Conditions muscles and bones while developing power and precision in strikes.
- **Tip:** Start with light strikes to avoid injury, gradually increasing the intensity as your body adapts. This prevents injury while allowing the body to strengthen over time.

Gichin Funakoshi, founder of Shotokan Karate,
practicing on a makiwara.

Core Strength

A strong core is essential for generating power, speed, and overall stability in martial arts. Without a solid core, your movements can lack the foundation needed to deliver forceful strikes and maintain balance.

- **Purpose:** Builds the foundation for power, speed, and balance.
- **Exercises:** Planks, Russian twists, and hanging leg raises.
- **Tip:** Incorporate core exercises into every training session to build a resilient base for all martial arts movements.

Sample Conditioning Exercises

These conditioning exercises are designed to build stamina, strength, and resilience, all of which are critical for martial arts training. They focus on both individual development and teamwork, encouraging mental toughness alongside physical growth.

· Knuckle Pushups

Knuckle pushups are a fantastic exercise for martial artists and athletes looking to strengthen their wrists, knuckles, forearms, and overall upper body while reinforcing proper alignment and conditioning for striking. They help build toughness in the hands, enhance grip strength, and promote wrist stability, which is crucial for punching power and injury prevention.

Benefits of Knuckle Pushups

1. **Strengthens Wrists & Forearms** – Reduces the risk of wrist injuries in striking.
2. **Knuckle Conditioning** – Builds calluses and bone density, useful for martial artists.
3. **Better Alignment** – Helps maintain proper wrist positioning for striking.
4. **Increases Upper Body Strength** – Engages chest, shoulders, and triceps.
5. **Core Activation** – Enhances balance and core stability.

Proper Form for Knuckle Pushups

1. **Positioning**
   a. Get into a standard pushup position.
   b. Place your fists on the ground, aligning them with your shoulders.
   c. Keep your knuckles flat, primarily resting on the first two knuckles (index and middle finger).
2. **Body Alignment**
   a. Maintain a straight line from head to heels.
   b. Engage your core and keep your elbows at about a 45 degree angle to your torso.

3. **Execution**
   a. Lower your chest slowly until it nearly touches the ground.
   b. Keep your fists stable and avoid wrist collapse.
   c. Push back up explosively to the starting position.
4. **Breathing**
   a. Inhale as you lower yourself.
   b. Exhale as you push up.

Variations and Progressions

- **Beginner:** Start on a soft surface (mat or carpet) or do them on your knees.
- **Intermediate:** Perform on a hard surface (wood or tile).
- **Advanced:** Use a weighted vest, elevate feet, or try one arm knuckle pushups.

Safety Tips

- Warm up wrists before starting.
- Avoid excessive pressure on the pinky or ring finger knuckles.
- Progress gradually to harder surfaces.
- If pain occurs, modify or rest.

· Four Person Pushups

Also known as group pushups or synchronized pushups, this exercise requires multiple people to perform pushups in perfect synchronization. This drill is great for building stamina, strength, and coordination while fostering teamwork.

- **Purpose:** Builds stamina, strength, teamwork, and coordination.
- **Tip:** Synchronization is key — ensure all participants move together to maximize the effectiveness of the exercise.

Students performing four person pushups.

Students performing three person pushups.

126

· Shinai Conditioning

Shinai conditioning involves using a bamboo sword (shinai) to toughen the body by targeting areas such as the shins, forearms, thighs, abdomen, and shoulders. This traditional training method is often used to build resilience and pain tolerance in martial artists.

In my school, we would begin with light taps, gradually increasing the intensity as the students' tolerance grew. I incorporated diaphragmatic breathing exercises to further enhance their mental toughness during this conditioning. The students enjoyed demonstrating their resilience, and the controlled nature of the strikes helped ensure no injuries occurred while still toughening the body.

During these sessions, students would often assume a horse stance position with their arms bent and fists on their hips. While in this stance, I would instruct them to practice diaphragmatic breathing exercises. As they exhaled, I would lightly tap the targeted areas with the shinai, gradually building their tolerance to impact. This exercise not only helped to strengthen their muscles and bones but also instilled a sense of confidence and mental toughness. I found that many kids enjoyed this practice, eager to demonstrate their strength and bravery.

- **Purpose:** Builds resilience and toughens the body by targeting key areas with light strikes.
- **Tip:** Focus on controlled, light strikes to prevent injury while gradually building durability. Practice horse stance and diaphragmatic breathing to strengthen both the body and mind during this exercise.

Conclusion

Traditional old school drills offer invaluable benefits for both mental and physical conditioning. From kata practice to makiwara training, these exercises build a solid foundation of discipline, technique, and resilience. Incorporating these time-honored methods into your training ensures you develop not only as a martial artist but also as a person — one who can face any challenge with determination and strength.

GM Vélez is using a shinai to condition Assistant Instructor Andy's abs.

GM Vélez is using a shinai to condition Assistant Instructor Raz's thigh.

GM Vélez is using a shinai to condition Apprentice Black Belt Henry's abs.

GM Vélez is using a shinai to condition Assistant Instructor Raz's arm.

Grandmaster Vélez is using a shinai to condition Master Charles Kim's abs.

This continuation of traditional old school drills brings in some highly effective blocking techniques and stances designed to build forearm strength, impact tolerance, and balance. These drills, combined with conditioning exercises, help practitioners develop the resilience and precision needed in martial arts. Below is an explanation of shinai conditioning, ensuring the techniques are easy to follow while emphasizing their purpose and benefits.

High Block Blocking Technique with Shinai

This exercise involves two practitioners, one holding a shinai and the other preparing to block. The goal is to condition the forearms while improving blocking accuracy and tolerance to impact. This drill is excellent for building defensive skills in a realistic setting.

Setup

- Practitioner 1 holds the shinai, standing in a front stance (left leg in front, right leg in back).
- Practitioner 2 faces them in a ready stance.

Execution

- Practitioner 2 steps forward into a front stance and performs a high block (left leg forward, right leg back).
- Practitioner 1 strikes Practitioner 2's forearm with the shinai as they block.
- Repeat this process 10 times, then reverse, stepping backward with the block.

Purpose

- Conditions the forearms, strengthening them to endure strikes. Builds tolerance to impact and improves blocking technique under realistic conditions.

Tip

- Ensure you're practicing with a partner who can provide consistent shinai strikes. Use controlled force and focus on precise blocking to simulate real combat scenarios.

2024 – (Left to Right): Grandmaster Vélez and Master Charles Kim conditioning the forearm with shinai.

2024 – (Left to Right): Grandmaster Vélez and Master Charles Kim conditioning the arms with shinai.

Horse Stance and Front Stance Workouts

Horse stance and front stance are foundational in traditional martial arts for developing leg strength, balance, and rhythm. These stances, though simple, are key to achieving stability and power in both striking and blocking techniques.

Purpose: Conditions the legs, strengthens the lower body, and enhances balance and core stability.

Tip: Hold the stance as low as possible, focusing on maintaining proper form. The lower you go, the more you engage your muscles, leading to better conditioning and balance.

Inside to Outside Blocking Technique (Horse Stance/Front Stance Workout)

This drill trains practitioners in executing inside to outside blocks, conditioning the arms while reinforcing balance and rhythm. The technique can be performed in both a horse stance and front stance, depending on the desired intensity.

- **Front Stance**
    - Both practitioners face each other in a front stance (left leg forward, right leg back).
    - The lead practitioner steps forward with a right inside to outside block while the second practitioner steps back and performs the same block.
    - Both arms strike on the outside of the other practitioner's arm.
    - Continue stepping forward and backward, performing the block for 10 repetitions.

    ↳ **Purpose:** Conditions the arms and it also improves rhythm, coordination, and timing in defensive movements.

ↄ **Tip:** Focus on strong, fluid movements. The goal is to match your partner's pace and strike together for optimal conditioning.

- **Horse Stance**
  - ○ Both practitioners face each other in a horse stance with their arms on their hips and hands in a fist.
  - ○ Begin by performing the right inside to outside block, striking together on the outside of the arm.
  - ○ Repeat the movement 10 times in place.

ↄ **Purpose:** Strengthens the arms, shoulders, and core while reinforcing proper stance and arm movements.

ↄ **Tip:** Keep your horse stance low and firm, focusing on stability. Make sure your blocks are crisp and accurate.

2024 – (Left to Right): Grandmaster Vélez and Grandmaster Moon Kim performing an inside outside block to condition the arms.

Outside to Inside Blocking Technique (Horse Stance/Front Stance Workout)

The outside to inside block drill is a counterpoint to the inside outside block, teaching practitioners to block strikes that come from the outer angle. This drill is performed in both a horse stance and front stance to engage different muscle groups while focusing on timing, arm conditioning, and defensive precision.

- **Front Stance**
    a. Begin in a front stance (left leg forward, right leg back).
    b. The lead practitioner steps forward with a right outside to inside block, while the second practitioner steps back, performing the same block.
    c. Both arms should strike together on the inside of each arm.
    d. Continue stepping forward and backward, performing the block for 10 repetitions.

    ↳ **Purpose:** Conditions the arms and develops proper defensive techniques to block outside strikes. Enhances balance and leg strength by incorporating footwork.|

    ↳ **Tip:** Concentrate on fluid motion and coordination with your partner. Aim to strike at the same moment for maximum conditioning and technical improvement.

- **Horse Stance**
    a. Both practitioners assume a strong horse stance.
    b. In place, begin with a right outside to inside block, making contact on the inside of the arm.
    c. Repeat the movement 10 times, alternating arms as necessary.

    ↳ **Purpose:** Strengthens the core and arms while maintaining lower body stability.

    ↳ **Tip:** As always, keep your stance low and grounded. Focus on precise arm movements to avoid excessive force while maintaining rhythm with your partner.

Conclusion

Traditional old school drills, such as high blocks with the shinai, inside to outside blocks, and stance training, are powerful tools for building both mental and physical toughness. These exercises condition the arms, forearms, and legs while improving coordination, balance, and endurance. By incorporating these foundational drills into your training, you not only strengthen your body but also sharpen your mind, developing the precision and resilience needed for high level martial arts performance.

Consistency in practicing these time-honored drills will help you gain an edge, transforming basic movements into powerful techniques that will serve you well in both sparring and self defense situations.

"Old school training doesn't ask if you're ready — it makes you ready. It doesn't build style; it builds substance."

— GM Raphael Vélez

Chapter 14: Breaking in Martial Arts: An Overview

Breaking refers to a powerful and precise technique in martial arts where a practitioner uses force, velocity, and technique to break a solid object, such as boards, bricks, or tiles. This practice serves both as a test of strength and as a demonstration of a martial artist's mastery over power, precision, and control. Breaking is an essential part of many martial arts disciplines, appearing in demonstrations, rank tests, and exhibitions.

Contrary to what some may think, breaking is not merely about raw strength — it is a science that involves proper alignment, speed, focus, and years of technical practice. When done correctly, breaking demonstrates a martial artist's ability to channel energy into a single, precise strike. It requires a combination of mental focus, physical conditioning, and correct form.

Breaking As a Test of Skill

Breaking tests are commonly used during belt advancement tests to gauge a martial artist's skill level, control, and precision. The difficulty varies based on the materials used and the techniques employed. Practitioners may use various strikes and kicks to break boards or blocks, showcasing their mastery of power generation and impact control.

My Personal Experience: Training and Preparation for Breaking

In preparation for breaking, I remember countless trips to Home Depot to buy patio blocks (2" x 8" x 16") with my teammates. We would set up across the street from our school in a municipal parking lot and practice breaking two to three times a month.

This was a regular part of our training routine, where we focused not only on power but also on refining our technique for precision. We also utilized rebreakable boards, which are a fantastic tool for consistent practice. These boards can be reused, making them a practical choice for repetition. Each color of the board — white, orange, green, blue, red, brown, and black — usually corresponds to belt rankings and degree of difficulty, providing a great visual representation of progression.

*Raphael Vélez practicing his power breaking technique
across the street from the school parking lot in
Naugatuck, Connecticut, in 2003. Breaking 13 patio blocks (2" x 8" x 15").*

*Raphael Vélez practicing his power breaking technique in Cheshire, Connecticut, in 2003,
breaking 13 out of 14 patio blocks (2" x 8" x 15").*

137

These drills not only serve as physical conditioning exercises but also carry cultural and historical significance within their respective martial arts styles. It's important to practice these drills under the guidance of a qualified instructor to ensure proper technique and safety. Additionally, modern training often integrates these traditional drills with contemporary approaches to create a well-rounded martial arts practice.

Breaking Techniques: Common Methods

There are several techniques used in breaking, each requiring unique skills in terms of alignment, focus, speed, and power. Below are some of the most widely practiced breaking techniques across various martial arts styles:

- **Palm Strike**

A highly effective technique, the palm strike involves using the heel of the hand to break a target. This method requires precise alignment between the hand, wrist, and forearm, along with sharp focus.

> ➜ **Key Focus:** Alignment, balance, and focused energy.
> ➜ **Tip:** Keep the hand open and fingers tight to transfer power through the palm effectively.

- **Fist Strike**

Using a closed fist, this technique is often applied with either a hammer fist or a vertical or horizontal punch. It emphasizes power generation from the core transmitted through a strong, tight fist.

> ➜ **Key Focus:** Knuckle conditioning, wrist alignment, and body mechanics.
> ➜ **Tip:** Be mindful of wrist positioning to avoid injury while maximizing force.

· **Knife Hand Strike (Chop)**

The knife hand strike is a classic technique, performed by striking with the edge of the hand. The fingers are held tightly together, and the strike is delivered in a precise chopping motion.

→ **Key Focus:** Accuracy, speed, and edge of hand conditioning.
→ **Tip:** Keep the fingers tight to form a strong, unified striking surface.

· **Elbow Strike**

The elbow strike is a powerful, close-range technique used to strike downward onto the target. Elbow strikes are highly effective due to the proximity of the body's core strength and the sharp angle of impact.

→ **Key Focus:** Power, accuracy, and arm positioning.
→ **Tip:** Generate force from the rotation of the torso to enhance the strike.

· **Knee Strike**

Similar to the elbow strike, knee strikes are shortrange techniques that can generate a lot of force. They are particularly effective for breaking boards or tiles held at midlevel heights.

→ **Key Focus:** Core power and speed.
→ **Tip:** Drive the knee upward with force, focusing on hitting with the lower part of the thigh for maximum impact.

Breaking Kicks: Techniques for Powerful Leg Strikes

Kicks are often used in breaking demonstrations, where precision and power must come together in perfect harmony. Below are some key kicking techniques used in breaking:

· Front Kick

A straightforward technique, the front kick involves striking with the ball or heel of the foot. It is one of the most powerful kicks used in breaking and requires proper alignment of the hips and legs.

- → **Key Focus:** Hip engagement, balance, and foot positioning.
- → **Tip:** Aim for a clean, sharp strike with the ball of the foot or the heel, depending on the target's height and strength.

· Side Kick

The side kick is performed by delivering a lateral strike with the heel or the edge of the foot. This technique is ideal for breaking boards positioned at mid to high level heights.

- → **Key Focus:** Proper hip rotation and alignment.
- → **Tip:** Focus on balance and precision when chambering the leg before the strike.

· Roundhouse Kick

A dynamic technique, the roundhouse kick involves a circular motion to generate force. It is executed by swinging the leg in a horizontal arc, striking with the shin or the ball of the foot.

- → **Key Focus:** Speed, rotation, and precision.
- → **Tip:** Maintain balance and aim to connect the shin with the target for maximum impact.

· **Axe Kick**

The axe kick is a downward strike where the foot comes down from above the target, striking with the heel, similar to the motion of an axe chopping wood. This kick is particularly effective for high level breaks, often used in demonstrations.

→ **Key Focus:** Power from height, accuracy, and downward force.
→ **Tip:** Aim to strike the target cleanly with the heel to maximize the downward force.

· **Spinning Back Kick**

The spinning back kick is one of the most powerful techniques in martial arts. It involves a full spin, where the practitioner strikes with the heel, generating force through speed and momentum.

→ **Key Focus:** Timing, coordination, and balance.
→ **Tip:** Proper foot positioning and rotational power are key to executing this technique effectively.

· **Flying Kicks**

Flying kicks are dynamic and visually impressive techniques often used in board breaking demonstrations. Here are some effective flying kicks for board breaking, along with tips on execution:

➤ **Flying Front Kick**
  ○ **Execution:** Jump off your back leg while pulling the front knee upward, extending the kicking leg forward to strike the board with the ball of your foot.
  ○ **Focus:** Speed, knee chamber height, and a strong snap at the point of contact.
  ○ **Best for:** Single or double board breaks, especially effective with thinner boards.

➢ **Flying Side Kick**

  ○ **Execution:** Run a few steps to build momentum, jump off the back leg, and drive the side kick forward, striking with the heel or the edge of the foot.

  ○ **Focus:** Hip alignment, body posture, and maintaining a strong chamber during flight.

  ○ **Best for:** Multiple boards or spaced boards, demonstrating power and control.

➢ **Jumping Roundhouse Kick**

  ○ **Execution:** Perform a jumping roundhouse by rotating your hips midair and striking the board with the instep or the ball of your foot.

  ○ **Focus:** Proper hip rotation, tight chamber, and controlled snap.

  ○ **Best for:** Speed breaks or angle breaks, showcasing precision.

➢ **Tornado Kick (360 roundhouse)**

  ○ **Execution:** Spin 360 degrees, jumping off one leg and striking the board with the other in a roundhouse motion.

  ○ **Focus:** Balance, rotational speed, and striking accuracy.

  ○ **Best for:** Demonstrating agility and control, often used in breaking routines for style points.

Old School Drills for Breaking Practice

The tradition of breaking often incorporates old school drills, designed to build foundational skills and mental resilience. These drills emphasize simplicity and time-tested techniques, helping practitioners hone their focus, concentration, and overall power. They also combine modern training methodologies, such as rebreakable boards and patio blocks, with traditional conditioning exercises.

Conclusion: The Mindset of Breaking

Breaking is far more than just a physical exercise — it is a test of mental discipline, focus, and technique. The power to break boards or bricks comes from years of dedicated training, proper conditioning, and a sharp mind that knows how to channel force effectively. Consistent practice, mindfulness, and a drive for improvement will help you refine your breaking skills and reach your potential as a martial artist.

I encourage every martial artist to embrace breaking as a part of their practice, both for the physical conditioning it offers and the mental discipline it fosters. Continuous improvement should be the goal, not just in breaking but in every aspect of martial arts training.

"Breaking is not about destroying — it's about revealing. Each shattered board uncovers the strength, focus, and spirit within."

— GM Raphael Vélez

Chapter 15: Mental Health in Martial Arts

Additional Resources for Special Populations

Martial arts training offers numerous benefits for individuals with mental health conditions and behavioral challenges, providing a structured environment that promotes discipline, respect, and self control. In this chapter, we will explore how martial arts can specifically help individuals diagnosed with attention deficit/hyperactivity disorder (ADHD), oppositional defiant disorder (ODD), conduct disorder (CD), and reactive attachment disorder (RAD). By offering practical tips and targeted strategies, martial arts can serve as a therapeutic tool for these populations, helping to address symptoms and promote positive behavioral changes.

· Martial Arts and Attention Deficit/Hyperactivity Disorder (ADHD)

ADHD is a neurodevelopmental disorder characterized by inattention, hyperactivity, and impulsivity. It often becomes evident in childhood and may persist into adulthood, affecting school performance, social interactions, and workplace productivity. Children with ADHD may struggle with focus, fidgeting, and difficulty controlling their impulses.

Benefits of Martial Arts Training for ADHD

- **Improved Focus and Concentration:** Martial arts involve structured routines and repetitive practice, which help children with ADHD improve their ability to concentrate on specific tasks.

- **Channeling Hyperactivity:** The physical activity in martial arts provides an outlet for excess energy, allowing students to channel hyperactivity into constructive movements.

- **Enhancing Self Discipline:** Martial arts emphasize the importance of following rules, waiting for turns, and practicing self-control, which helps children with ADHD manage their impulsivity.

Practical Tip

- **Consistency Is Key:** Establish a regular training routine that provides structure and predictability for children with ADHD. Clear instructions and consistent practice can help them develop the focus and discipline they need.

· Martial Arts and Oppositional Defiant Disorder (ODD)

ODD is characterized by persistent patterns of angry, defiant, and disobedient behavior, especially toward authority figures. Children with ODD often engage in frequent arguments, refuse to comply with rules, and may exhibit irritability and anger.

Benefits of Martial Arts Training for ODD

- **Respect for Authority:** Martial arts schools emphasize respect for instructors, fellow students, and the rules of the dojo. This structured environment can help children with ODD learn to respect authority in a positive way.

- **Emotional Regulation:** Through martial arts, students learn techniques to manage their emotions, helping them to better cope with frustration, anger, and irritability.

- **Positive Behavior Management:** Martial arts offer opportunities for positive reinforcement, where students are rewarded for good behavior, focus, and effort. This helps reinforce desirable behaviors.

Practical Tip

- **Teamwork and Cooperation:** Incorporate group activities and partner drills that foster teamwork and cooperation. This helps children with ODD practice working with others and builds a sense of community and mutual respect.

· Martial Arts and Conduct Disorder (CD)

Conduct disorder is a more severe behavioral condition involving persistent patterns of aggressive behavior, property destruction, deceit, and rule violations. Children with CD may engage in physical fights, destroy property, and show a lack of regard for the rights of others.

Benefits of Martial Arts Training for CD

- **Promoting Nonviolent Conflict Resolution:** Martial arts training teaches students how to handle conflicts without resorting to violence. By practicing controlled sparring and learning self defense, children can develop appropriate responses to conflict.

- **Instilling Respect and Discipline:** Through martial arts, students learn to respect others, follow rules, and take responsibility for their actions.

- **Building Empathy:** Roleplaying exercises and scenario based training can help children with CD develop empathy as they learn how to understand the perspectives and feelings of others.

Practical Tip

- **Role Playing for Empathy:** Use roleplaying exercises to simulate conflict situations where students must demonstrate self control, empathy, and appropriate responses. This helps children with CD develop emotional awareness and social skills.

· Martial Arts and Reactive Attachment Disorder (RAD)

RAD is a condition in which children struggle to form healthy attachments with caregivers, often due to early neglect or abuse. Symptoms include difficulty forming emotional bonds, a lack of positive emotions, and social withdrawal.

Benefits of Martial Arts Training for RAD

- **Building Trust and Positive Relationships:** The consistent structure of martial arts classes helps children with RAD build trust with instructors and peers. Supportive, positive interactions during training foster healthy attachments.

- **Boosting Self Esteem:** Martial arts training is goal oriented, offering children with RAD achievable goals, such as mastering a technique or advancing in rank. This boosts their self esteem and confidence.

- **Developing Social Skills:** Training in a group setting allows children with RAD to interact with others in a safe, supportive environment, helping them develop crucial social and emotional skills.

Practical Tip

- **Create a Nurturing Environment:** Ensure the martial arts setting is nurturing and supportive, where students feel safe to express themselves and build positive relationships. Encouragement and positive reinforcement are key to fostering trust and emotional growth.

Summary of Diagnoses and Martial Arts Benefits

Martial arts training can offer numerous benefits for children and adolescents with Attention Deficit/Hyperactivity Disorder (ADHD), Oppositional Defiant Disorder (ODD), Conduct Disorder (CD), and Attachment Disorder. Here's a summary of how martial arts can be beneficial for each of these conditions:

This table summarizes the key symptoms of ADHD, ODD, CD, and RAD and highlights how martial arts can address these challenges:

Foundational Skills for ADHD, ODD, CD, and RAD

This table summarizes the key symptoms of ADHD, ODD, CD, and RAD and highlights how martial arts can address these challenges:

Diagnosis	Key Symptoms	How Martial Arts Help
ADHD	Inattention, hyperactivity, impulsivity, poor academic performance, difficulty following directions, low frustration tolerance	Improves focus, self control, physical activity, goal setting, emotional regulation
ODD	Argumentative/defiant behavior, anger/irritability, vindictiveness, blaming others, frequent temper tantrums	Teaches positive behavior management, respect for authority, conflict resolution, emotional stability
CD	Aggression, destruction of property, deceitfulness or theft, serious rule violations, lack of remorse	Promotes nonviolent conflict resolution, respect, personal responsibility, empathy
RAD	Difficulty forming attachments, decreased positive emotions, unpredictable behavior, difficulty seeking/accepting comfort, lack of social interaction	Builds trust, boosts self esteem, provides structure, teaches coping skills, develops social skills

Foundational Skills for ADHD

This table summarizes how martial arts can benefit children with ADHD.

Symptom	Description	Benefit of Martial Arts
Inattention	Difficulty sustaining attention in tasks or play activities	Improved focus and concentration
Hyperactivity	Excessive fidgeting, running, or climbing in inappropriate situations	Physical activity to channel excess energy
Impulsivity	Interrupting or intruding on others, difficulty waiting for turns	Self-discipline and self-control
Poor academic performance	Careless mistakes, failure to finish tasks	Goal setting and achievement, boosting self esteem
Difficulty following directions	Frequently fails to follow through on instructions	Structured environment with clear rules and routines
Low frustration tolerance	Easily frustrated, quick to anger	Emotional regulation and stress management techniques

Foundational Skills for ODD

This table summarizes how martial arts can benefit children with ODD.

Symptom	Description	Benefit of Martial Arts
Argumentative/ Defiant behavior	Often argues with authority figures, refuses to comply with requests	Positive behavior management and respect for authority
Anger/Irritability	Often loses temper, easily annoyed, resentful	Anger management and emotional regulation
Vindictiveness	Spiteful or vindictive behavior	Conflict resolution skills
Blaming others	Blames others for their mistakes or misbehavior	Self-discipline and personal responsibility
Frequent temper tantrums	Intense outbursts of anger and frustration	Structured environment and emotional stability

Foundational Skills for CD

This table summarizes how martial arts can benefit children with CD.

Symptom	Description	Benefit of Martial Arts
Aggression toward people/animals	Bullies, threatens, or intimidates others; initiates physical fights	Nonviolent conflict resolution and self-control
Destruction of property	Deliberate destruction of others' property	Respect for others' belongings through structured discipline
Deceitfulness or theft	Lies, steals, or breaks into property	Personal responsibility and integrity
Serious rule violations	Stays out at night, runs away from home, truancy from school	Structured routine and respect for rules
Lack of remorse	Shows no guilt or regret for actions	Emotional regulation and empathy development

Foundational Skills for RAD

This table summarizes how martial arts can benefit children with RAD.

Symptom	Description	Benefit of Martial Arts
Difficulty forming attachments	Trouble forming emotional bonds with others	Building trust and positive relationships
Decreased positive emotions	Difficulty experiencing joy, happiness, or positive emotions	Boosting self-esteem through achievements
Unpredictable behavior	Inconsistent and challenging behavior	Structured and predictable environment
Difficulty seeking/ accepting comfort	Unable to seek or accept comfort when distressed	Developing coping skills and emotional regulation
Lack of social interaction	Avoids social interaction, seems detached	Social skills development and sense of belonging

"The true fight in martial arts is not against an opponent, but against the chaos within. Mental health is the silent kata we practice daily."

— GM Raphael Vélez

Left to right: Raphael Vélez Rivera and his father, Miguel Rivera, at the Navarre Beach Fishing Pier.

Parents: Herda M. Rivera and Miguel A. Rivera.

Grandmaster Vélez began writing his book in 2023 inside this shed owned by his father. The picture on the top shows the office space he built within the shed, where the journey of bringing his book to life first began.

2024 –GM Vélez (left) and GM Moon Kim (right).

2024 –GM Vélez (left) and GM Moon Kim (right) wearing their official Kummooyeh uniforms.

GM Vélez (left) with GM Joung Bouk Soo, founder of the World Kummooyeh Federation, South Korea.

GM Vélez received his World Kummooyeh Federation certification from GM Joung Bouk Soo.

2023 – Former President of the Korea Taekwondo Moo Duk Kwan Association, GM Jong Hwan Lee (9th Dan), with GM Vélez after awarding him his 8th Dan.

2023 – GM Fred Kouefati (9th Dan), President of Global Legendary Taekwondo (formerly Richard Chun Taekwondo Moo Duk Kwan), with GM Vélez (right) after awarding him his 8th Dan.

Left & Right: GM Vélez and GM Song Ki Kim (MDK #312), founder of the World Dang Soo Do Union (WDU).

2024 – From left to right: GM Moon Kim, GM Kyong Duk Lee, GM Pedro Vangas Jr., GM Pete F. DeFosses, and GM Vélez in Bogotá, Colombia.

2024 – From left to right: GM Vélez and GM Kyong Duk Lee (88 years old), 9th Dan Kukkiwon Taekwondo and founder of the first Taekwondo school in Colombia.

From left to right: Dr. Robert Goldman (physician, surgeon, 5th-degree black belt, and world champion strength athlete) with GM Vélez at the Hall of Fame.

Photo above and below: American martial artist and actress GM Cynthia Rothrock with GM Vélez at the Hall of Fame.

Northern Virginia black belt instructors (left to right): Elizabeth Hernandez, Chris Barker, Sara Arias Shanks, Raphael Vélez, Nic Khoo, Razvan Nae, and Andrew McCarthy.

(left to right): Elizabeth Hernandez, Razvan Nae, GM Vélez, Andrew McCarthy, Nic Khoo, Henry McCarthy, and Jamey Wyman.

GM Vélez and Sara Arias Shanks, the first Black Belt in Northern Virginia.

Early 1980's GM Vélez performed a double split kick at a seminar.

Northern Virginia black belt instructors (left to right): Andrew McCarthy, Jamey Wyman, and Razvan Nae.

Late 1980s – GM Vélez performing a double split kick at the Cheezic Tang Soo Do School in Waterbury, Connecticut.

1990 – GM Vélez performing a pole vaulting flying kick at Cheezic Tang Soo School, Waterbury, Connecticut.

1985 –Raphael Vélez with legendary martial artist Dan Inosanto, best known as the foremost protégé of Bruce Lee and a key figure in the development and preservation of Jeet Kune Do (JKD).

1984 – Former World Kickboxing Champion Bill "Superfoot" Wallace (left) and Raphael Vélez.

1984 – Waterbury, Connecticut: From left to right – Marcel Beaulieu, former Heavyweight World Kickboxing Champion, Joe Lewis, and Raphael Vélez.

1990 – Waterbury, Connecticut: Don Belsito and Raphael Vélez training at the Cheezic Tang Soo Do School.

2015 – Tang Soo Do Master Alliance Banquet: From left to right – Larry Bergamo, Don Belsito, and Raphael Vélez.

The inset photo was taken in Moscow, Russia, in 1990.

Master Vélez performing a Bo form at a fundraiser in the early 2000s.

Cheshire: Home of Concrete-Breaking World Champs

by Sara Savage
Herald Staff

There is something fascinating unfolding on West Main Street. Master Ralph Bergamo, a seventh degree black-belt and owner of Bergamo's Personal Training and Wellness Centers in Cheshire and Naugatuck, has been involved in martial arts for 30 years. He is bringing his team of self-defense and concrete block-breaking masters to the World Championship Mr. Olympia Contest in Las Vegas on October 18. On July 4 and 5, Team Bergamo competed in the U.S. Open at Disney World, winning several first and second place titles. Bergamo himself won first place in black-belt self-defense.

Breaking is a combination of technique, focus, and belief in oneself. "Concentration and the use of one's whole mental and physical ability" is the key to breaking according to Bergamo. Breaking training begins with breaking wood and moves onto breaking multiple boards, eventually advancing to the concrete blocks.

"Breaking is a practice that one can learn to harness personal adrenaline, focus on objects and break them," says Bergamo. At the Mr. Olympia Contest, contestants will be evaluated by seven world-class judges and use a variety of different body parts to break

the concrete patio blocks. "You set up as many blocks as you think you can break, and try to break them with a single strike," Bergamo explains.

Winners are those who break the number of blocks nearest to the amount they set out to break, not those who simply break the most.

The level of danger in breaking largely depends upon one's state of mind. Bergamo has witnessed people breaking their arms and feet in competitions. "Mental training becomes like instinct, like when a parent is able to lift a car off of their child," Bergamo says. Team Bergamo prides itself upon its mental intensity and finds it necessary in order to perform its amazing feats. One can feel their camaraderie and intensity.

Team Bergamo consists of four men: Master Bergamo of Cheshire, Master Clinton Murphy of New Milford, and Master Drew Serrano and Master Raphael Velez of Waterbury. The team holds seven world titles in breaking and self-defense. In addition, they have choreographed some of their breaking and self-defense demos to music, which is a unique and innovative idea in the world of martial arts.

Serrano has been involved in martial arts for 22 years, and joined Bergamo's as an instructor and

Photo by Sara Savage
l. to r.: Master Drew Serrano, Master Ralph Bergamo, and Master Raphael Velez continue to honor Grand Master Joeseph Rossi, who passed breaking along to them 25 years ago. Not pictured: Master Clinton Murphy.

coordinator in 1998. He owns Training Systems, a company that specializes in bodyguarding, and is now involved with the stunts and fight scene choreography for a movie in New York.

Velez has been a martial artist since 1973, and is a longtime friend of Bergamo's. He came in fifth in power-breaking at the U.S. Open and is in the Eastern U.S. International Martial Arts Association Hall of Fame, along with Bergamo.

Murphy is highly recognized and has been in martial arts for 13 years. He took second place in power breaking at the Open this year and 1st place in self-defense at the 2001 Open. He has been within the top three in nearly every major breaking tournament.

Bergamo and Velez will compete in Las Vegas as lightweights (200 lbs. and under), and Serrano and Murphy will compete as heavy weights (200 lbs. and up). The

four men are among the approximately 15 contestants from around the world who were invited to compete in the Mr. Olympia Contest. The contest draws a huge crowd and is televised on ESPN. Team Beragamo will take at least one world title. If he wins, Bergamo will retire from breaking.

"It is an honor for the school, the town, and the state," Bergamo says of the team's inclusion in the Mr. Olypmia Contest.

Newspaper article: Team Bergamo – Breaking Champions from Cheshire, Connecticut.

Raphael Vélez (left) and Drew Serrano (right) on top of a high rise in New York City, working as stuntmen for a film.

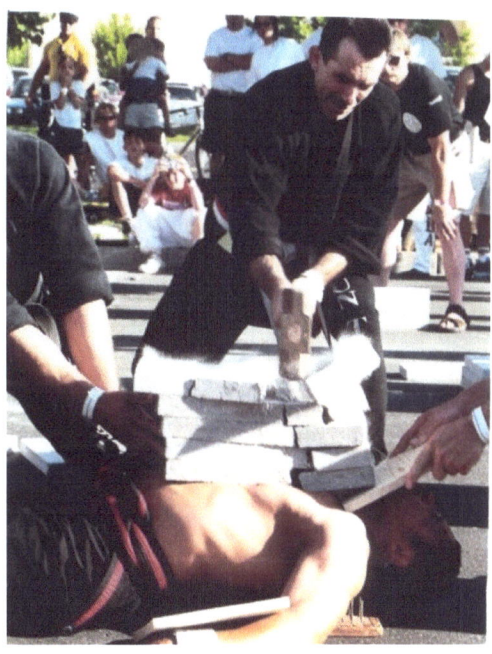

GM Vélez lies on a bed of nails while GM Bergamo breaks five patio blocks with a sledgehammer on his chest at the 2000 World Championship in Las Vegas, Nevada.

GM Vélez breaking 10 flaming boards at the 2000 World Championship in Las Vegas, Nevada.

Team Bergamo congratulates Raphael Vélez after his victory at the 2004 U.S. Open ISKA World Championship.

*Raphael Vélez celebrating and dancing the night away after winning
the 2004 U.S. Open ISKA World Championship.*

ISKA Power Breaking Triple Crown Champion
Light Weight Division 2004

Raphael Vélez performing his signature break, a pole vaulting flying kick,

on July 4, 1998, at Naugatuck High School in Connecticut.

Raphael Vélez working out on a bicep machine in 2005 while training in California for a world record event.

Raphael Vélez smashing 13 patio blocks to win the 2004 U.S. Open ISKA World Martial Arts Championships — setting a new record and raising the standard for lightweight competitors.

Raphael Vélez broke 13 patio blocks to win the 2004 U.S. Open ISKA World Martial Arts Championships, setting a new standard and record for lightweight competitors.

Clinton Murphy and Raphael Vélez after winning the heavy and light weight 2003 Power Breaking United States ISKA Championship in Las Vegas, Nevada.

Raphael Vélez performing a speed break on four scallop blocks at the 2002 U.S. Open ISKA World Championship.

Colin Thompson breaking 15 blocks and setting a new heavyweight world record at the 2004 U.S. Open ISKA World Martial Arts Championships.

Former World Champion Mike Reeves presenting the 2003 Power Breaking United States ISKA Champion belt to Raphael Vélez in Las Vegas, Nevada.

Raphael Vélez and Colin Thompson with their lightweight and heavyweight belts at the 2004 U.S. Open ISKA World Martial Arts Championships.

Team Bergamo Schick Quattro at the Action Martial Arts Mega Weekend at Tropicana Casino, Atlantic City.

Team Bergamo Schick Quattro with former UFC Middleweight Champion Frank Shamrock.

Team Bergamo Schick Quattro with UFC World Champion Frank Shamrock and World Champion Kickboxer GM Bill "Superfoot" Wallace.

Hall of Fame event at the Action Martial Arts Mega Weekend at Tropicana Casino, Atlantic City. From left: GM Vélez, World Champion GM Frank Shamrock, and World Champion GM Bill "Superfoot" Wallace.

Fernando Camareno, with his eyes covered, performing a jumping back kick to break scallop blocks.

2004 – Fernando Camareno and Raphael Vélez in San Juan, Puerto Rico, with his International Sport Karate Association Triple Crown Championship belts.

Larry Fields, a multi-time world champion and distinguished martial artist, is renowned for his exceptional skills in competitive breaking. He became one of Master Vélez's most respected mentors in the art of power breaking.

Raphael Vélez (left) with former Mr. Olympia Jay Cutler at the Arnold Classic.

Left to right: Raphael Vélez with his brothers Carlo, Rafael, and Jorge.

Master Vélez at the range conducting an AR15 class.

Master Vélez at the range conducting a pistol class.

Left to right: GM Vélez and Coast Guard Divemaster Berry diving a shipwreck in the Florida Keys, 2004.

GM Vélez at Pensacola Beach has completed over 400 dives with SSI. He is a Divemaster Assistant Instructor and has been exploring the world's oceans for more than 20 years.

ABOUT THE AUTHOR

Master Raphael Vélez began his martial arts training at the age of 10, earning his junior black belt in Taekwondo (ATA) in his teens. In 1978, his family moved to Connecticut, where he began training in Tang Soo Do under Grandmaster Walter J. Belsito Sr. (MDK #17029). During the early 1980s, he trained under the legendary pioneer Grandmaster Robert Cheezic (MDK #2278) until the mid1990s. He completed most of his master ranks under Grandmaster Walter J. Belsito Sr. until his passing in 2013.

Throughout his martial arts career, Master Vélez has trained with some of the greatest martial artists in the world. Now an 8th Dan and one of the highest-ranking instructors in Tang Soo Do and the Korea Taekwondo Moo Duk Kwan Association worldwide, he is a martial arts legend with over 50 years of experience. He has mastered multiple disciplines, including Tae Kwon Do, Tang Soo Do, Filipino martial arts (Kuntao), and boxing.

As a multiple-time International Sport Karate Association (ISKA) World Champion, Vélez is particularly renowned for his power breaking skills, holding a competition record for breaking 16 concrete blocks with his elbow. He also achieved the prestigious ISKA Triple Crown Championship in power breaking, securing titles such as the U.S. Open ISKA World Martial Arts Championships, North America ISKA Championship, and United States ISKA Championship. Through his dedication, skill, and mental toughness, Master Vélez continues to inspire martial artists worldwide.

Beyond his martial arts career, Master Vélez has been a dedicated mental health professional for 27 years. He holds degrees in drug and alcohol rehabilitation counseling, general science, and psychology, and completed his master's degree in clinical mental health counseling. His unique approach integrates his expertise in firearms training, mental health therapy, and martial arts, teaching students the importance of discipline, focus, and resilience.

When he's not coaching or teaching martial arts, Master Vélez is an NRA/USCCA certified firearms instructor, conducting professional firearms training. Additionally, as a professional Divemaster with Scuba Schools International (SSI), he often explores the world's oceans, embracing adventure both above and below the surface.

2004 Master Velez in his official Team Bergamo Schick Quattro uniform.

Martial Arts Biography book by Ted Gambordella, published in May 2023.

The Art of Mental Toughness

184

185

www.ingramcontent.com/pod-product-compliance
Lightning Source LLC
Chambersburg PA
CBHW040854120626
46551CB00001B/13